T0035471

THE ASTRO CHIMPS

America's First Astronauts

DAWN CUSICK

CHICAGO
REVIEW
PRESS

Published by Chicago Review Press Incorporated
814 North Franklin Street
Chicago, Illinois 60610
ISBN 978-1-64160-895-4

Library of Congress Control Number: 2023930790

Interior design: Sarah Olson

Printed in the United States of America
5 4 3

astro: From the Greek word *ástron,* meaning star; see "astronomy" and "astronaut."

chimps: Great apes from the forests of western and central Africa known for their intelligence, personality, and close relationship to humans; abbreviation for chimpanzee.

astrochimps: The highly trained young chimps who beta tested America's Space Race technology; America's first suborbital and orbital astronauts. Newspapers coined the term *astrochimps*; the animals were also called "chimponauts" and "space chimps."

CONTENTS

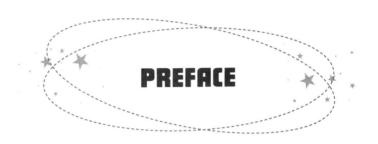

PREFACE

In the mid-1960s, Dr. Bill Britz took a bus tour of Cape Canaveral with a friend. The veterinarian had looked forward to revisiting his space work. As the bus drove around the sunny cape, past launchpads, control rooms, and booster rockets, the tour guide dazzled everyone with facts and stories. But the guide didn't mention the piece of history Dr. Britz knew best: the space chimps. The guide had never heard of the astrochimps, even though they were America's first astronauts.

Today, stories about space chimps in cartoons, video games, and TV shows are everywhere. These tales are usually science fiction, which makes sense to people who didn't live through the Space Race of the 1950s and '60s. Young chimps ride on their moms' backs in the wild, right? Not in airplanes or spacecrafts! Sending chimpanzees to space sounds absurd now.

But the 1960s were a different time. People believed that the astrochimps would make space safe for humans and help America beat the Soviets in the Space Race.

Looking back on this era in history makes us ask new questions. Do we have the right to take something just because we want it? Surely, we can steal a sandwich if we're starving. But is it OK to take wild chimps from their forest homes so they can test-drive rockets?

We cannot undo the past, but we can create a new future. We can promise to treat animals, including highly intelligent ones like chimpanzees, with dignity. We can protect their wild habitats. We can care for captive chimps. And we can promise to remember the astrochimps because their story is *not* fiction.

WILD LIVES

Deep in the tropical forests of French Cameroon, thousands of chimpanzees snuggled into treetop nests. Fresh-cut leaves made soft pillows. Some chimps fell right to sleep. Others stayed awake for a while, listening for lions and staring at the stars.

One night, the stars shared the sky with something new. Sputnik, the world's first satellite, passed overhead every 98 minutes. A month later, the Soviet Union launched a second satellite with a small dog named Laika aboard.

Maybe the chimps saw the satellites. Maybe not. But one thing's for sure: the chimps had never seen a dog before. They didn't care about outer space—it wasn't part of their territory. They cared about predators. And venomous snakes. And large birds that stole their figs.

On the other side of the world, radar screens confirmed the news: the Soviets had beaten the United States to space. Americans stuttered in fear and confusion. Could Soviet satellites spy on the United States? Drop atomic bombs? Why didn't the United States have satellites?

Americans hovered over shortwave radios, listening for a signal, waiting for the satellites to come into range. Sputnik went *beep-beep-beep* three times a second, while Sputnik II bragged "Look at me!" in a high-pitched whine. US engineers fast-tracked a satellite, but it exploded on the launchpad in a fireball of humiliation nicknamed Flopnik.

To compete in the Space Race, the United States needed powerful rockets. It also needed spacecrafts and information about how space might affect the people who rode in them. Would outer space make human blood boil? Or pop eyeballs from their sockets? Could human brains work in zero gravity and strong g-forces?

For answers, the country turned to chimpanzees. *Yes, really.*

Life in the Wild

The forest chimps didn't understand the Space Race, but they did understand competition. And war. *Who has the most power? The best skills?* The chimps asked these questions all the time, answering with huus, barks, and grunts. They spoke with gestures, too, tattling on troublemakers and thieves, plotting revenge, and making up with hugs and kisses.

In every chimp troop, some animals had more power than others. Large males gained status by winning battles and respect. With the right friends and clever schemes, smaller males also became leaders.

Dominant chimps liked to remind everyone they were the boss. All the time. They pounded trees. Stomped their feet. Slapped and kicked other chimps. And if they felt ignored? Look out! They chased guilty apes through the woods in a swirl of dust and screams.

Low-ranking chimps tried hard to avoid trouble, greeting leaders with special grunts and peace presents such as sticks and rocks. For young chimps, dominance was tricky. Fight faces and play faces looked the same when they ambushed adults with handfuls of twigs and dirt, or played keep-away games with food. Moms hovered nearby, ready to rescue their silly toddlers at the last moment.

But even the strongest, smartest chimps couldn't protect their young from the new animal claiming dominance: *humans*. Local people killed chimps for bushmeat and medicines, while poachers caught chimps in nets baited with fruits and nuts and sold them to buyers around the world.

A Wild New Home

In 1957, the same year the Sputniks launched, a Florida man bought a few dozen small chimpanzees from

French Cameroon poachers. Alton Freeman packed his chimps in wood crates and loaded them onto a cargo plane for the flight across the Atlantic Ocean. Six thousand miles later, the chimps arrived at the largest bird farm in the world. That's right, a *bird farm*.

Brochures and billboards advertised the Miami Rare Bird Farm as "a paradise for camera fans." Penguins, flamingos, toucans, spoonbills, macaws, cockatoos, cranes, powder puff ducks, swans, king vultures, storks, honeycreepers, and ostriches decorated the lawns and trees with bright colors and sounds.

The chimps knew some birds from Africa, but the birds from Asia, Australia, India, South and Central America, and Antarctica looked odd. Another strange bird roamed the Miami Rare Bird Farm, too: tourists from northern states called "snowbirds" flocked to the farm by the thousands, trading their icy winters for warm Florida sun.

Confused, the chimps explored their new home. They'd never smelled an ocean, or hot dogs and suntan lotion. And nothing stayed the same. One day bears and buffalo passed by; the next day, alligators and sloths. Cheetahs, antelope, tapirs, and anteaters? Oh, yeah. Circus tigers and elephants wintered at the farm, and animal actors retired there when Hollywood stopped calling.

Other animals came and went as Alton Freeman traded with zoos and brokers. Recently, the US government had become a good customer. Freeman kept the news hush-hush, as ordered, but the army sent two of his monkeys, Able and Baker, on a short space trip. Maybe some Miami Bird Farm chimps would go to space?

Soon, the new chimps became part of a family business. Freeman, his wife, Frances, and their three children, Teresa, Cliff, and Dolly, lived on the farm. Frances Freeman taught them circus tricks, and the chimps did four shows a day, costarring with parrots and llamas.

Some chimps lived with the family inside their house. Between shows, the chimps came home to play, sidestepping the paradise cranes that followed Frances

Frances Freeman tours the Miami Rare Bird Farm with parrots and a chimp. *Alton Freeman, State Library and Archives of Florida, Florida Memory Collection*

Freeman everywhere. At night, the drama shifted to the kids' bathroom where a Brazilian otter refused to share the tub, and then to the couch where a small gorilla snuggled his way to the best spot in front of the TV.

The rest of the chimps lived behind a tall waterfall, posing for tourist photos and studying the humans, especially the little ones. The shyest chimps hid in coconut trees, watching the ruckus below—kids chasing runaway penguins and kangaroos; zebras barking at neighbors who dared to mow their lawn; a gorilla yelping when the phone rang. It was all a bit much.

Astrochimps in Training

Two years later, Alton Freeman sold 25 chimps to the government for a top-secret project. Most chimps flew to Holloman Air Force Base in New Mexico, a few miles from the country's atomic bomb test site. A few chimps went to the University of Kentucky first. *Goodbye, bird farm! Hello, space camp!*

When the Miami Bird Farm chimps arrived, they met chimps from US zoos and animal farms, plus some chimps who came straight from Africa. Many chimps were under three years old. Some were much younger.

Young chimps were easier to teach and more likely to accept humans as leaders. Just as important, they would fit inside a spaceship. The very best would become astrochimps in the Mercury Chimpanzee Training Program. Their job? Testing everything America needed to make space travel safe for humans: rockets, spacecrafts, breathing air, gravity, and more. If the Mercury program succeeded, the first astronaut in space would be American.

At first, the chimps didn't look much like astronauts. They bounced off the walls in a chorus of chaos: hooting, barking, grunting. They squabbled with strangers, shrieked at spiders—air force officers stared in disbelief. These big-eared jokesters were America's secret weapon in the Space Race?

Sergeant Ed Dittmer, the lead chimp trainer, tried not to ask questions.

"A lot of things at the time were classified, and the less you knew of classified, the easier it was to keep it classified," he recalled. Instead, the sergeant focused on his new assignment. He'd spent the previous two years at Holloman sending people to the edge of space with giant air balloons in Project Man-High, and then sending mice to space on Able rockets in Project Mouse-in-Able. This chimp work might be more fun.

New chimps spent their first six weeks in quarantine so they would not spread viruses and parasites. Veterinarian Bill Britz ran the quarantine unit. At night, while his own toddlers slept in their warm beds, Dr. Britz cared for sick chimps in Holloman's hospital. "Chimps that came from animal farms and zoos were usually very healthy. But animals coming directly from Africa were often sick or very thin, and needed medicines, fluids, food, and 24-hour care," Dr. Britz recalls. (Many times, poachers didn't feed the chimps well, and it could take weeks or months to find buyers.)

Dr. Britz was new to chimpanzees too. He had trained with dogs and cats, not apes, and had no idea how much chimps needed each other. "One night, one of the chimps grabbed the leg of another and would not let go, so I housed them together," he says. "They were close to death when I left that night, but the next morning they were bright-eyed and barking hellos at me. After that, I paired up the other chimps, and we never lost another baby again."

After quarantine, the first round of tryouts began. Chimps flew in fighter jets for four hours a day. Trainers studied their faces, watching for fear when engines made loud sounds and vibrations. Most chimps loved the jet rides, pounding their armrests and hooting in glee.

A few chimps refused to go again, standing their ground outside the jets. There was no point in forcing them on the plane. Astrochimps needed to like flying. Some chimps struck a bargain with trainers: half a candy bar before the flight and the other half after.

The next round of tryouts looked for chimps who could handle strong g-forces and zero gravity (0 g). On Earth, about 1 g of gravitational force keeps people on the ground. Without this force, everything on Earth would float into space. When a spacecraft enters space, the force from its rocket engines fights Earth's gravitational pull.

To test the chimps with g-forces, air force pilots brought three or four chimps at a time on parabolic flights. Sergeant Dittmer organized the trips on C-131 transport planes. First the plane powered into the sky at a 45-degree angle. At about 30,000 feet, the pilot sent the plane into a diving arc—a parabola—and everyone on board felt weightless for 30 to 45 seconds. As the plane

Tiger returning from a training flight. These flying classrooms let trainers see how the chimps handled loud noises, strong g-forces, and microgravity. *US Air Force, Holloman Air Force Base Photographic Branch*

pulled out of the dive, everyone inside felt 6 g. Roller coasters use the same physics to give riders a thrill with a few seconds of 4 or 5 g at the bottom of hills and during banking turns, and a moment of 0 g at the start of sheer drops.

The chimps usually did a dozen parabolas per trip, one after another. But some days they did thirty! Dr. Britz sat with the chimps, ready to give medical care if a chimp passed out. The human passengers often got airsick when they hit 0 g and left the plane clutching white paper puke bags, according to Dr. Britz. "But I never saw a single chimpanzee vomit on those parabolic flights."

Holloman's airport staff marveled at the daily parades of chimps getting on and off the planes. Usually, the air force used C-131s for medical emergencies and moving VIPs (very important persons). When the chimps flew, control tower workers called them VIPs: very important primates.

Chimps who passed motion sickness tests advanced to the next tryout: sitting alone in a small room. Mercury spaceships would be nothing like the high-tech space stations depicted in science fiction movies or even the International Space Station. Imagine, instead, traveling in a tiny kitchen cabinet.

Claustrophobic chimps need not apply.

Research Subjects?

Officially, scientists and trainers called each astrochimp by a number. The National Aeronautics and Space

Administration (NASA) also used these numbers. In technical reports, they called the chimps "the subject" or "the flight animal."

NASA's staff argued that the space chimps should *only* have number names. If something went wrong in a test flight, an astrochimp's death would bring negative publicity to America's space program, especially if the chimp had a cute name. The air force psychologists didn't want to nickname the astrochimps either.

Soon, however, the lead veterinarian, Dr. Jerry Fineg, noticed the astrochimps' unique personalities. He also noticed how much trainers were bonding with them. "We had to be careful not to make pets of them," he explained. "Four- to five-year-old chimps are very similar to a four-year-old child." Sternly, Dr. Fineg reminded everyone that the astrochimps were research subjects, not pets or children. Do *not* humanize them.

Dr. Fineg and NASA officials may have wanted workers to view the chimps as research subjects, "but that didn't last long," Dr. Britz says, laughing. Vets and trainers carried the baby-faced chimps on their hips, nuzzling their cheeks and tickling their feet. Who could resist those cute little pot bellies and freckled faces? One veterinarian drove chimps around the campus in an old crash-test ambulance—oh, how the chimps *loved* to ride.

How could they not humanize the chimps when the chimps acted so *human*? Chimps copied human gestures as they worked, tapping their fingers on their chins, the way some people do when learning a video game or pondering a new idea. Chimps shrugged their shoulders and rolled their eyes.

The chimps often looked human too. After flight tests one day, a pilot scooted an astrochimp into the copilot seat as he taxied his plane to its parking space. Then the pilot leaned down to hide. When ground workers glanced up, they saw a very serious chimpanzee in the cockpit window, steering the plane right toward them.

"Some chimps paid a lot of attention to nearby adults and mimicked their behavior," Dr. Britz remembers. "If a chimp noticed a trainer sucking on lemon drop candy from their pocket, the chimp wanted a lemon drop. One chimp was legendary for saluting. When a superior officer came into the training area, he stood in line at attention, holding the salute for as long as the humans did. No one taught him to do that—he just noticed the behavior and copied it."

The air force trains people to follow orders, but everyone ignored Dr. Fineg. *Baby Face! Big Ears! Miss Priss! Double Ugly! Big Mean!* Trainers just couldn't resist giving the chimps names. One bouncy chimp saw trainers play-boxing during breaks, and soon the chimp boxed. And then he was Rocky, after world-champion boxer Rocky Graziano. One chimp's sweet, happy face reminded trainers of Disney's Minnie Mouse, so they named her Minnie. Another chimp loved blankets, so trainers named him Linus, after the blanket-carrying little boy in the *Peanuts* comic strip.

Numbers 64, 65, and 85 became Duane, Ham, and Billy—named for their veterinarians. Family and friends inspired new names for Rosie, Glenda, and Frances. (Goodbye, Numbers 8, 106, and 108!) Trainers named Bridget and Grace after movie stars. Enos received a more serious name: *Enos* means "man" in Hebrew and "one" in Greek.

A Lot to Learn!

Soon, the best chimps began formal astronaut training. Astrochimp schedules looked like school days without homework. At 7:30 AM the chimps ate breakfast: chimp

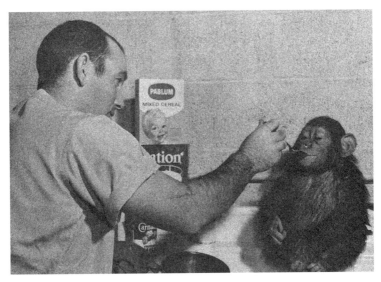

Astrochimps feasted on chimp cocktails and fresh fruit for most meals. What's in chimp cocktail? Baby cereal, milk, chimp chow, Jell-O, and soft-boiled eggs. Yum. Here, a trainer feeds breakfast to Baby Face. *US Air Force*

chow mixed with milk, baby cereal, Jell-O, and soft-
boiled eggs, plus a fresh grapefruit or orange.

After breakfast, the chimps went to exam rooms,
where veterinarians measured weights, pulses, blood
pressures, respirations, and temperatures. Vets checked
the chimps' eyes, noses, ears, and mouths, too, on the
lookout for viruses and other infections.

Sergeant Dittmer stood near exam tables during
exams, trying to distract the chimps so the vets could
work. Some chimps played with the stethoscopes and
blood pressure cuffs, listening to human hearts. Ham
preferred to play with the sergeant, grooming his curly
hair for insects and undoing the buttons on his shirt.

Enos refused to play. Instead, he crouched his head
low, fine-tuning his about-to-pounce glare on anyone
who met his gaze. Vickie nuzzled her head against Dr.
Britz during checkups, tucking her hands under the vet's
arms while the Sergeant scratched behind her ears.

The chimps finished each checkup by drinking a cup
of raspberry Jell-O mixed with vitamins and antibiotics,
and eating a dried banana treat.

Next, trainers dressed the chimps in diapers and
space suits. On their ride to school, curious chimps
entertained themselves by removing their diapers and
jackets. They dressed and undressed their neighbors,
placing the garments upside down and sideways until
they figured them out.

Other chimps spent the school ride playing with the
padlock on the truck's back door. They'd studied the

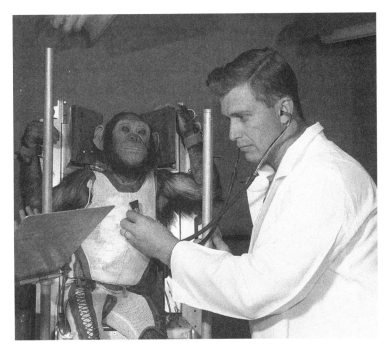

Dr. Bill Britz listens to Elvis's heart. Astrochimps received checkups before and after each training session and full physicals each month. The chimps expected lemon drop candies or banana pellets as rewards after every checkup. *US Air Force, Holloman Air Force Base Photographic Branch, Texas A&M University Libraries*

way the human hands moved over the lock. How hard could it be? One day, a chimp figured it out. He flung open the doors, "waving and jabbering" to cars passing by. When the truck stopped, the chimps jumped out. Such fun! Trainers followed, chasing the chimps across the desert. That night, trainers moved the padlock to the outside of the truck.

Once at school, the trainers brought the chimps to the "Bored Room." "We would set them about four or five feet apart so they couldn't reach each other and play," Sergeant Dittmer said. For new students, sitting alone in a chair for five minutes seemed impossible.

The chimps ate fruit as they sat there, waiting, waiting, *w a i t i n g.*

Chimps glanced between their neighbors and the humans. Can't we play a game? *Any* game? Nope.

Slowly, trainers increased the chair time until the chimps could sit alone for a few hours. "Finally, we could set them there all day, and they'd just sit there and play [by themselves]," said Sergeant Dittmer.

Other chimps started training at the University of Kentucky. A news story called "Chimps No Chumps" shared details from Dr. Karl Lange, who ran the program:

> Let me tell you, we had a lot of fun. . . . First we tried handling them like students. We made friends with them. It didn't work. They made friends all right. They ate our bananas and played with us for hours. But when it came time to work, they acted like spoiled children.
>
> Then we tried setting rules—just like campus rules. We set a time schedule and stopped giving them free run. . . . Some rebelled. Some couldn't take it and others wouldn't. But most became A and B students.

After the chimps learned to sit in chairs, trainers placed panels with lights and levers in front of them. *Wahoo—toys!* Trainers let the chimps play with the equipment and gave them banana treats when they pressed levers. It took more than a pound of pressure to press a lever.

Chimps are natural scientists, testing things out and remembering what works. Wild chimps use stones as hammers to open nuts, and sticks to scoop ants and termites from their nests. Some chimps use leaves to collect drinking water.

Soon, trainers added blue and white lights in different shapes. Before long, the astrochimps knew colors, shapes, and numbers. *How?* By watching their trainers. In the wild, young chimps learn fast this way, memorizing how to weave nests and find food while riding on their moms' backs—just by paying attention.

Class Dismissed!

At 3:30 PM, classes ended. The chimps rode buses back to the exam rooms for posttraining checkups. And then, finally, the chimps could ditch their uniforms. *Ahhhh.* Dr. Vernon Pegram remembers being "one of the lucky trainers who got to clean the chimps' mesh training suits every day." It was a very messy job!

For dinner, the chimps feasted on more chimp chow and fruit, plus a high-protein smoothie made with raw eggs, Jell-O, milk, and powdered baby cereal.

Chimps enjoyed free time after dinner. Their cages opened onto an outdoor playground lined with small shrubs and desert sand. Minnie spent her time mothering younger chimps, teaching them games and how to peel fruits. Enos searched for bugs—they had a crunchy crisp you couldn't get from banana pellets. Other chimps relaxed by grooming, running their fingertips through a neighbor's hair to find insects and parasites.

Vickie followed Sergeant Dittmer around while he did chores. (Vickie had been a family pet in Paris, so she knew about housework.) Vickie carried the water bucket and helped scrub the walls. Then she and the sergeant shared a treat.

Even Dr. Fineg joined the after-school fun. One day, the doctor climbed into a chimp cage, just for giggles. And there he sat, in his shiny boss shoes and perfectly gelled hair, peeling a banana. Ham studied Dr. Fineg for a moment—*Hmmm, that looks about right, but he really should share that fruit*—then leaned in for a drink from the cage's water fountain.

At night, trainers took turns hanging out with the chimps. Psychologists wanted every chimp to know every trainer. Vernon Pegram didn't mind the extra chimp time. Before he came to Holloman, Dr. Pegram, with French scientists, studied sleep in wild baboons. Building trust with the astrochimps was much harder.

Most chimps didn't mind the extra people time. The chimps knew which trainers carried candy, and put their hands out, expecting them to share. Ham didn't ask for treats. He just waited until the trainers were busy and then slipped his hand into their pockets, padding around until he found lemon drops or gum.

Dr. Fineg checks out a new view while Ham gets a drink. When the veterinarian first started working with the astro-chimps, he warned workers not to get too friendly with the young chimps. *US Air Force, New Mexico Museum of Space History*

Trainers brought tricycles and other toys to the nightly visits. For some chimps, people made the best toys: they were so easy to tease. Rocky savored the nightly visits, plotting new ways to wrangle the water hose from the person on cleanup duty. Chimps gathered around the nightly show, cheering and cackling as water pummeled a trainer's face. Soon, more trainers would rush in, and a grand game of tug-of-war began. Rocky always won.

Test Time

After a few months, the astrochimps started taking tests. After all, what's a school without exams? These weren't paper and pencil tests. Instead, the astrochimps did screen tests on panels in front of them. When a blue light near their left hand blinked, chimps had five seconds to press the left lever. When a white light near their right hand flashed, they had 15 seconds to press the right lever.

For correct answers, chimps got a treat: a dried banana pellet or a sip of water. For wrong answers, they got a light shock on their foot. Dr. Britz says the shock felt more like a vibration: "It was a mild shock, strong enough to get the chimps' attention, but not strong enough to hurt them. You could hold the shock plates in your hands without dropping them."

In another test, chimps received a banana pellet if they pressed a lever *exactly* fifty times. Forty-nine times? No banana. Fifty-one times? No banana. Wrong answers reset the machine, forcing the chimps to start over.

The astrochimps were not learning lights and levers so they could pilot spacecrafts. Instead, NASA would use the tests to compare the chimps' classroom scores to their scores in space. If their performance stayed the same or went down just a little, NASA could assume that human astronauts could think clearly in space. Trainers also measured how fast the chimps answered questions. This data would tell NASA whether space would change a human astronaut's reflexes.

At first, the chimps pressed their levers superfast, *bangity-bangity-bang*. When they got close to 50, the chimps slowed down: 46, pause, 47, pause, 48, pause, 49, pause. Before pressing the final, 50th lever, the chimps moved a hand under the dispenser to catch their banana treat. Air force workers were gobsmacked. Who knew chimpanzees were this smart?

A reporter who watched a training session said the chimps moved their levers so fast that they looked like pinball players. One chimp pressed 7,000 levers in 70 minutes, making just 28 mistakes for a score of 99.9 percent!

Cupcake set the speed record, pressing her levers 7,200 times in 45 minutes. Cupcake only used her right hand and made just 15 errors. (She kept her left hand free for collecting banana treats, of course.) Bobby Joe and a few other chimps pressed levers with their feet, leaving both hands free to grab treats.

To test the astrochimps on circles, triangles, and squares, engineers programmed a computer to light up three shapes on the panel. For each test, two shapes were

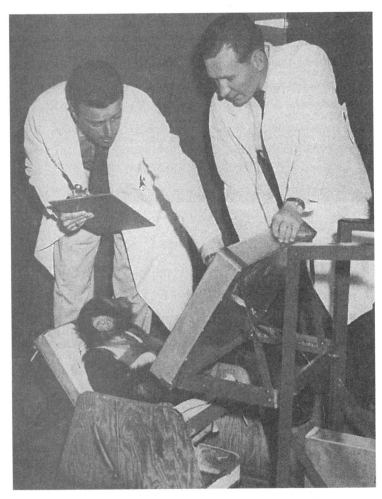

Five days a week, the astrochimps took tests on shapes, colors, and counting. Chimps answered questions by pressing a lever under the correct answer with more than a pound of force. Astrochimps surprised engineers when the chimps found mistakes in the circuits. By pushing buttons and levers in new combinations, the chimps tricked the computer into giving them extra treats! *US Air Force*

the same and one was different. If two triangles and one circle appeared, chimps pressed the lever under the circle.

Vickie dazzled people with her amazing shape skills. The astrochimp could do 72 shape tests in a row without making a single mistake *and* without even glancing at the screen. How did Vickie take tests without seeing the questions? Simple: the computer program shuffled the shapes and the questions, and Vickie memorized the order. "Vickie looked like she was playing the piano when she did those tests," says Dr. Britz.

Vickie loved using her shape skills to play tic-tac-toe. When politicians and military brass visited the astrochimps, they often played a few games with her. "If you gave Vickie the first move, she beat you every time," Dr. Britz adds.

Minnie memorized the shape questions too. One day Minnie stunned visitors while taking an even harder shape test. First a shape flashed on Minnie's screen. A second later came a circle, triangle, square, and dash. To get the right answer—and banana treats—she pressed the lever under the shape that matched the first screen. Minnie studied the people instead of her screen, answering questions from memory. Dumbfounded visitors stared in awe. Then they tried taking Minnie's tests— and failed. They couldn't answer fast enough.

But classes didn't always go smoothly. Sometimes, chimps dissolved into screams and flailing feet, just like human temper tantrums. And who could blame them? By chimp standards, the astrochimps were still children.

In the wild, young chimps ride on their mom's back, not in spacecrafts. They stay with their moms for at least five years and don't become adults until their mid-teens.

Building Skills

In January 1959 the Soviets launched a small spacecraft called *Luna 1*. Destination? The Moon. *Luna 1* missed its target, but only by a few thousand miles. In the fall, the Soviets tried again with *Luna 2,* which crashed *into* the Moon. The next month, *Luna 3* took the world's first photos of the mountains on the far side of the Moon. The Soviets weren't just dreaming about the Moon. They had already sent spacecraft there.

NASA gave the Air Force Chimpanzee Training Program new goals and deadlines. America's space plans would stay on the ground unless the astrochimps' test scores went up. But the humans at Holloman still had a lot to learn about teaching chimpanzees.

For the chimps, their social lives mattered. A lot. They spent long hours in classrooms and labs, and they could not test well sitting next to a chimp they didn't like—or one they liked too much. The same held true with the humans. Chimps sassed trainers who annoyed them and worked harder for trainers they liked.

To solve the problem, psychologists played a grand game of mix and match, switching chimp seats and trainers to discover who did best near whom. Minnie, Elvis, Miss Priss, Big Ears, and Baby Face came to Holloman a year before the others, so they knew each other's quirks.

Ham, Enos, Rocky, Duane, Jim, Billy, and George lived together for more than a year and a half at the Miami Rare Bird Farm. Tiger, Enos, and Sam trained with each other at the University of Kentucky. It wasn't easy!

Some astrochimps disliked all humans, or perhaps didn't respect the humans as leaders. "One day," says Dr. Britz, "Dr. Fineg was leading Enos around outside on a leash and Enos bit him on the rear end . . . just to let him know he was there." Enos also bit Sergeant Dittmer's fingers, and Duane bit his veterinarian's leg. "When we worked with Fred, we had to be careful or he would jump right in your face." The trick with these chimps was finding the human they disliked the *least*.

Once psychologists found the best chimp and human teams, test scores went up.

For 18 months—day in, day out—the astrochimps continued space training. Chimps who did well on lever tests spent extra hours in the air, on C-131 air force planes. Their training chairs and light panels traveled with them so they could do lever tests in the air. Pilots raced the "flying classrooms" through turbulence, steep turns, and climbs. Could chimps concentrate on their lever work when the environment around them changed? Psychologists and trainers needed to know. So did NASA.

The answer? Oh yes, they sure could.

To gain more g-force experience, the astrochimps trained in machines called centrifuges. A space-training centrifuge looks like a wild combination of a science lab centrifuge and a high-flying amusement park ride with a large steel ball on the end of a 50-foot steel arm. Trainers belted chimps inside the metal ball, and then a 4,000-horsepower engine spun them at high speeds. Ready to throw up yet?

The centrifuge changed angles too. Astrochimps could face 8 g of force while right-side up and 14 g a few seconds later when upside down. Confused about the difference? A 100-pound person feels 800 pounds of pressure against their bones, muscles, and skin in 8 g; 14 g feels like 1,400 pounds of pressure. G-forces can move eyeballs, blood, and even the heart. It can push, pull, and tear skin and muscles. Vision blurs. Colors turn gray. As it becomes harder to breathe, the brain can't get enough blood, and astronauts pass out.

Chimp trainer Vernon Pegram often sat in the slower centrifuge seat. His assignment? Study the chimps' responses to g-force changes. Some days, he volunteered to sit in the chimp seat so scientists could compare his body's responses to the chimps'. Dr. Pegram remembers "going faster and faster until my vision narrowed and then went black."

The Big Plan

While the astrochimps trained for space trips, human astronauts trained too. From more than 1,000 applicants, NASA invited 110 military pilots for the wildest job interview of their lives. Pilots went by numbers, not names, in test notes.

Just like the chimps, the pilots loved to compete. Who flew the newest fighter jets? Who held the most speed records? Who made the most aircraft-carrier landings? They also compared training details. Who handled the strongest g-forces? Who got the highest grades in rocket class?

After hundreds of tests, NASA chose the Mercury Seven astronauts: Alan Shepard, John Glenn, Virgil "Gus" Grissom, Malcolm "Scott" Carpenter, Gordon Cooper, Donald "Deke" Slayton, and Walter "Wally" Schirra.

Soon, the human astronauts were famous. They toured rocket factories. A south Florida car dealer gave them shiny new Corvettes, which they raced down the beach. The astronauts posed for photos and gave press interviews. The country wanted to know everything about the brave people who would help the United States beat the Soviets.

Unlike the astrochimps, the Mercury Seven knew what they were doing and why. NASA's job description had spelled it out. In short, the human astronauts would do everything needed to help the United States explore and conquer the dark, cold mysteries of space. They would train every day, learning to handle motion, force, and fear. If the chimps had seen the job details, they might have smashed bananas in protest.

To prepare for space, the human astronauts trained with the same machines the astrochimps used. They worked in chambers with high heat and humidity. The human astronauts trained in centrifuges, too, describing the machines as "dreaded" and "diabolical." John Glenn said, "You were straining every muscle of your body to the maximum . . . if you even thought of easing up, your vision would narrow like a set of blinders, and you'd start to black out."

NASA studied test results after each training session, and soon life turned into one big contest for the human astronauts. Winners would get spaceflights. Losers would stay home. The mood tensed even more when rumors spread that NASA had sorted them in two groups. NASA placed their favorite astronauts on the Gold Team: Alan Shepard, Gus Grissom, and John Glenn. Everyone else went on the Red Team.

Pad Leader Guenter Wendt, who worked with both the chimpanzee and human astronauts, recalled the stressful days. "Many times," Wendt wrote in his autobiography, "Ham held up better than our human subjects did during their tests."

One day, Wendt hit a nerve when he mentioned the astrochimps to astronaut Alan Shepard: "During one particularly long trial, I remember Shepard complaining and moaning. Finally, in exasperation, I told him, 'If you don't like it, I've got someone else who will do it for bananas.'"

No Girls Allowed

For the human astronauts, competition was everywhere. First, they fought each other for NASA's attention. They all wanted spaceflights.

America's astronauts also battled with Soviet cosmonauts. Who was braver? Better trained? More loyal to their country? Even their titles caused debate. The Americans were astronauts, from the Greek words *ástron* for "star" and *nautes* for "sailor," making them star sailors. The Soviet cosmonauts were also sailors, but they sailed the whole universe, not just the stars. (The Greek word *kosmos* means universe.)

And, *argh*, the Mercury Seven competed with those rowdy chimpanzees too. And now women wanted in on their deal? Could women really steal their seats?

In 1960, 13 female pilots endured three rounds of mental and physical astronaut tests with a NASA doctor. Like the Mercury Seven, they spent hours in the Vomit Comet and the wind tunnel and did hundreds of breathing and balance tests. Some women scored higher than the male astronauts. Oklahoma pilot Jerrie Cobb, who had flown more than 10,000 hours in 64 different types of planes, beat the men's record for time spent in an isolation tank by more than three hours. Before long, two more female pilots beat Cobb's record!

Even though the women were licensed pilots—many with thousands of flight hours under their belts—NASA said no. The women were not *military test pilots*, so they could not be astronauts. The Soviets liked this new Space Race and invited women to become cosmonauts. One leader bragged to the world, "There is no discrimination between the sexes in our science programs."

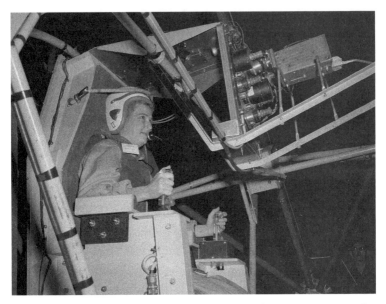

Pilot and astronaut-hopeful Jerrie Cobb during a test in the gimbal rig. The rig measured how well pilots could handle spins, tumbles, and rolls. *NASA*

Engineering the Science

While the chimpanzee and human astronauts trained for space, engineers and technicians worked too. So many problems to solve, so much pressure. NASA's Space Task Group surprised many young engineers by inviting them to brainstorm with high-ranking scientists. Claiborne Hicks said, "I was going to the Cape for a meeting with the Air Force, all these highfalutin' guys. Here I was a little pipsqueak engineer. I think I weighed about 110 pounds, and pimples all over my face. . . . I was the perfect nerd-type little guy."

As the shock of the Sputnik satellites wore off, politicians and military leaders realized something important: if countries fought the Space Race with science instead of bullets, the United States would need more scientists. Pronto! In a change called the Sputnik Effect, the government told schools across America to teach more engineering, chemistry, biology, and math. Schools got new textbooks, and teachers added more lab experiments to science classes.

To defeat the Soviets, the United States also needed reliable rockets, but NASA's early rocket tests were fiery failures. The first Atlas rocket exploded 32,000 feet above the launchpad. As one astronaut said, *"Wham!* It just blew up." The air filled with smoke, and large chunks of metal fell from the sky.

NASA tried again with a newer booster rocket. At first, the launch looked good. The rocket lifted a few inches off the ground. Then the engines shut down. The booster rocket collapsed, but the escape-tower rocket kept going. Without a booster rocket and spacecraft to guide it, the escape rocket "went berserk over the Florida sky, spitting flame and wreaking havoc." Loudspeakers warned people to "run for cover."

Failure was part of the process, though, as it always is in science. Each test launch helped NASA improve future trips. Failures were data points.

Another big problem to solve was how to control the astronaut's flight environment. Could astronauts survive the intense heat caused by friction? (Wait, you don't know about friction heat? Rub the palms of your hands together as fast as you can for a minute—did they warm up? Imagine the friction heat generated by a high-speed spacecraft moving through the air at more than 5,000 miles per hour. Friction heat can rise to 600 degrees Fahrenheit during space travel!)

Engineers had to invent a way to cool two places: the air inside the spacecraft's cabin and the air inside the astronaut's space suit. There was more to the environment than temperature, however. Astronauts needed oxygen to breathe and a way to remove the carbon dioxide and water vapor they exhaled. Space suits also needed to "trap the solids" if an astronaut puked. Engineers used vegetable soup to test the solids trap.

American scientists wondered how the Soviets were handling these challenges. Space Race spies from the Central Intelligence Agency (CIA) learned the answer: the Soviets were testing algae as an oxygen-creating solution. The CIA's Office of Scientific Intelligence shared the top-secret info with NASA. The algae could take in a cosmonaut's exhaled CO_2 and water and release O_2 for breathing through photosynthesis. No machines needed. US engineers pondered the Soviet's algae plan but decided it wouldn't work—too much algae would be needed. (The Soviets later came to the same conclusion.)

And then a new problem arose. Captain Chuck Yeager, a famous test pilot who broke the speed of sound barrier in an X-1 rocket plane, kept telling the truth. Every time Captain Yeager set a new speed record, reporters asked him if he wanted to be an astronaut. He would say, heck no, he didn't want to be an astronaut.

What? People crinkled their noses and shook their heads. *Who wouldn't want to be an astronaut?*

"I've been a pilot all my life," Captain Yeager sputtered in disgust, "and there won't be any flying to do in Project Mercury."

Captain Yeager had said aloud what most people didn't understand. NASA would fly the Mercury space capsule from the ground with remote control. *Huh?* Even reporters were confused.

"Well," Yeager responded, "a monkey's gonna make the first flight."

The Mercury Seven astronauts cringed. They did not want to be called passengers—or monkeys. They were *pilots*. Quickly, they campaigned to change the capsule's name to *spacecraft*. The astronauts also wanted windows and manual pilot controls added to the spacecraft. Great, sighed the engineers: more work.

By the end of 1960, NASA's Space Task Group solved its rocket problems. Engineers had also invented an environmental control system (ECS) to handle air in the spacecraft. NASA had tested the ECS on human pilots, but not at the altitudes needed for space travel. Now, the ECS needed to be tested in space.

It was time for a chimpanzee trip.

The Final Cut

In January 1961 NASA chose six "flight ready" astro-chimps for their skills and personalities. Ham, Enos, Minnie, Tiger, Rocky, and Roscoe made the cut. All six still had white cottontail tufts where a tail would be if they were monkeys. The chimps flew with their train-ers—and America's hopes and dreams—to sunny Cape Canaveral, Florida.

Once at the Cape, Sergeant Dittmer split the chimps and their trainers into two groups. Trainers even cooked their food in different kitchens. NASA couldn't risk one sick chimp infecting the others and delaying the mission.

During the early days of the Space Race, human and chim-panzee astronauts lived and trained in Hangar S at Cape Canaveral Air Force Station in south Florida. They may have worked in the same building and on the same equipment, but the human astronauts went out of their way to avoid the chimps. *NASA*

Vernon Pegram stayed with his star students, Ham and Minnie. By now, the chimps and their trainers were well bonded, and NASA didn't want strangers disturbing the chimps or their work.

Hangar S became their new home. (Hangars are large, garage-like buildings that protect airplanes from bad weather.) The air force had renovated Hangar S into a three-story workspace with offices, medical labs, training areas, and bedrooms for the human astronauts.

For more than a year, the human astronauts had practiced spaceflights in Hangar S. This was *their* territory. So was testing new aircraft. Why were the chimps even here? Alan Shepard called the astrochimps "a great circus act." If NASA grounded the chimps, Shepard said, it would "kick-start the program," making him first in space.

But engineers and scientists would not budge. They insisted the chimps live and work in the same place as the human astronauts to make the chimps real beta testers. Astrochimps and their trainers lived on one side of Hangar S.

Veterinarian Bill Britz remembers, "The human astronauts did not like following the chimpanzees. They did not want anything to do with the chimps. One day, I got a call from the head flight surgeon, asking me if I could come down and get a blood sample from one of the Mercury Seven astronauts. I said yes, I had time, but reminded him, *'I'm a chimpanzee veterinarian.'* Luckily, a nurse showed up, so I didn't have to do it. Gus Grissom was a neat guy and wouldn't have given me any grief, but some of the others would have been upset to have a veterinarian draw their blood."

During the day, the Mercury Seven avoided the astrochimps. They missed Tiger's intense stare, like an ambush predator, crouched low and ready to pounce. They didn't see Minnie's long, graceful arms, wrapped around a trainer's neck, or Rocky resting on a trainer's hip, snuggled under his chin. They never saw Duane, "a mature fellow," calmly doing his space work, or Ham and Enos flying through test questions, pulling levers at warp speeds.

The human astronauts tried to avoid Chuck Yeager's insults too. But the famous test pilot's words kept creeping through their minds: "I don't want to fly anything where you have to sweep the monkey crap off the seat before you sit down."

At night, the Mercury Seven could not escape the astrochimps. To get to their bedrooms, the human astronauts had to pass by the chimp quarters. The long hallway smelled like unflushed toilets. Alan Shepard felt "assailed by hoots, screeches, screams, and howls."

Before long, six of the seven human astronauts refused to sleep near the astrochimps. "In the end we decided the humiliation of stepping aside for a monkey was bad enough. We certainly didn't have to live with the howling dung-flingers." They packed their suitcases in a huff, moving to a nearby hotel. Colonel Glenn stayed at Hangar S. He could work harder without the nightly parties and fans demanding autographs. *Anything* John Glenn could do to win the top astronaut spot was worth living with chimps.

Test Runs

As the astrochimps adjusted to life at sea level, 4,000 feet lower in elevation their last home in New Mexico, the chimps began training in new conditions. They now worked levers in flight couches instead of chairs. The human astronauts also had couches.

From aluminum layered in hexagon shapes NASA made each couch to custom fit specific chimps and humans. The couch design was not random. From hundreds of crash-test experiments, engineers knew that this design absorbed the most energy at impact.

Both the humans and the chimps would travel in space suits. The human astronauts knew they should not break the pressurized seals in their space suits. But how could NASA keep curious chimps from undressing in space? They decided to cover the astrochimp's couch with a lid. (Imagine a toddler's car seat covered with a metal lid with a window.) The environmental control system would work inside the sealed couch the same way it would inside a human astronaut's space suit. And chimps could still move their hands and arms for lever tests.

To prepare for space, the astrochimps started working inside full-size plywood replicas of spacecrafts, complete with control panels and lights.

As the lead trainer, Sergeant Dittmer helped the chimps work. He also answered questions from engineers and scientists and studied veterinarian reports

Ham working levers in his custom couch. During spaceflights, the couch's lid would form a tight seal around the astrochimp. *NASA*

twice a day. But Dittmer's biggest job now was keeping the astrochimps calm. And the best way to do that was to keep the trainers calm.

The astrochimps studied their trainers much more than they studied shapes, colors, and numbers. They knew when one of their humans was nervous: the small muscles around their eyes twitched in a new way, or their words came in a different pitch. The sergeant kept the reporters at a safe distance, trying to make the days feel normal.

Everyone toiled long hours. So much was at stake. News stories made the astrochimps' roles crystal clear: without successful chimp flights, human flights would never happen, and the United States would never catch the Soviets.

Soon, NASA's staff started rehearsing transportation plans. Hangar S was a few miles from the launchpad, so the chimps and their trainers drove back and forth, every day, until NASA knew exactly how long each step took. In between trips, trainers placed Ham and Rocky on the hoods of trucks and cars and let them sit at the wheel.

Practical jokes eased the intense stress. "One day," says Dr. Britz, "we took Minnie in her couch out to the launchpad for another dry run. We had to stop at a guard station to show our security badges when we went on and off the base. On the return trip, we took Minnie out of her couch and placed her in the front passenger seat. After the guard checked my credentials, he

Ham behind the wheel of a truck a few days before America's first suborbital spaceflight. Times were tense, and humor eased the stress. *US Air Force*

looked over at Minnie, and his eyes got big. A few days later, the guards came over with security badges for all of the chimps!"

As the clock ticked toward launch day, it was time to make big astrochimp decisions. Twenty-seven hours before liftoff, all six chimps began a low-bulk diet: 15 food pellets, some fruit, and a little water.

A few hours later, NASA chose two finalists: Ham and Minnie. Later that evening, the lead veterinarian and psychologist studied both chimps, ranking them by skills and personality. When they compared notes, Ham topped both lists.

A head cold or temper tantrum would send Minnie to space instead.

ASTROCHIMPS
IN SPACE

For suborbital spaceflights, NASA chose Redstone missile rockets. As the Redstone's engine burned liquid fuel, it generated 78,000 pounds of thrust. The rocket's thrust would serve as the booster, propelling the 64,000-pound rocket and the 2,000-pound spacecraft upward, against gravity.

In suborbital flights, the spacecraft (and the astronaut!) return to Earth in an arch-shaped trajectory. "The suborbital flights . . . have a 'loft' trajectory, like throwing a ball into the air," explained astronaut John Glenn.

At the launchpad, a large steel scaffold, called a gantry, let hundreds of technicians and engineers service the rocket and the spacecraft. The Redstone gantry used a hammerhead crane to move the spacecraft from its delivery truck to the top of the rocket. Pulleys helped move large equipment and heavy tools, and NASA built platforms at different heights, creating safe places to work. To get to the top of the gantry, workers rode a rickety old elevator.

Launchpads were busy places during the early Space Race. Above, the cherry picker's crane aligns its bucket with the Mercury spacecraft. *NASA*

The night before the flight, as the astrochimps slept nearby, technicians filled the Redstone's fuel chamber with an explosive mix of liquid oxygen and alcohol. Next, they added the pyrotechnics, then the hydrogen peroxide thrusters.

Just before liftoff, NASA would drive a large, crane-like rig called a cherry picker to the launchpad. The cherry picker featured a crane mounted to the back with a bucket at the end. (Electric and cable companies use high-tech versions of this invention to safely work high in the air.) Technicians would raise the crane by remote control, aligning the bucket with the spacecraft's side door. If there was a last-minute fire or other emergency, a human astronaut could blow the door hatch and escape into the bucket. The crane would swing away from the launchpad as the cherry picker raced to safety.

NASA tested and retested each part of the flight plan. At liftoff, the Redstone booster rocket would power Ham's spacecraft upward, roaring with thunder-like sounds and vibrations. Ham and the other astrochimps trained with these intense roars and trembles. NASA did not want the launch to surprise or frighten the chimps on mission day.

At a set point in the atmosphere, smaller rockets would detonate, pushing the spacecraft *off* the rocket. Then, without thrust, Ham would feel weightless. From the ground, Mission Control could use small fuel jets to turn the spacecraft up, down, sideways, or all the way around.

Another group of rockets, called retro-rockets (reverse rockets), would work like brakes, slowing down the spacecraft's reentry speed as it fell back to Earth.

A few minutes later, two parachutes would open. The first parachute, called a drag chute, would open when Ham was a few miles above the ocean. This parachute would slow and steady the falling spacecraft. When Ham was about 10,000 feet from the water, the spacecraft's main parachute would open. This larger parachute would soften the astrochimp's landing.

To absorb more splashdown force, a landing bag and the heat shield would extend below the spacecraft by about four feet. On impact, the bag and heat shield would work together to help the spacecraft float upright. At the last minute, engineers added fiberglass fabric to the heat shield, hoping to make landings less dangerous. Ham's flight would test-drive this new solution.

Recovering an astrochimp or a human astronaut from the ocean after splashdown was the last big problem to solve. NASA went to the army for helicopters. "We could handle that much load, but we don't know how to operate off [aircraft] carriers," said the army, "and we hardly ever fly over water. So maybe you ought to talk to the navy." But the navy said no. Its helicopters were "pretty well maxed out with antisubmarine warfare equipment."

"The third stop," explained helicopter pilot Wayne Koons, "was the Marines." They practiced recovering spacecrafts along southern Florida beaches and rivers, following "the spacecraft up and down the waves."

Every part of the plan had to work. The astronaut's life depended on it.

Countdown

On launch day, January 31, 1961, Ham and Minnie's trainers woke them up early.

By 1:15 AM, the chimps sat on exam tables, getting physicals. Next, veterinarians placed biosensors on Ham and Minnie. The sensors would measure temperature, pulse, and breathing rate when they were in space. Then, veterinarians taped electrodes onto the chimps' chests and legs to collect heart data. After hundreds of dress rehearsals, today felt normal to the astrochimps.

Trainers dressed Ham and Minnie in diapers and waterproof pants. The countdown clock read T-minus 9 hours, 36 minutes.

Pad Leader Guenter Wendt called the countdown clock a "monster." Technicians, engineers, and others worried about everything. During a countdown, a test conductor calls out hundreds of items from a checklist. People responsible for each item answer with "GO" if their part is ready, or "NO GO" if it's not. There are no maybes. A "NO GO" puts everything on hold.

Can you imagine finishing your school day with a countdown clock? Instead of the dismissal bell ringing at an exact time, you would work through a checklist.

Lunchroom clean? *GO*. Homework assigned? *GO*. Intercom announcements made? *GO*. Buses ready for travel? *NO GO*. Waiting . . . wondering . . . waiting . . . would your countdown clock start over or pick up where it left off? At NASA, the answer depended on the problem.

At 2:03 AM, Sergeant Dittmer and a technician moved Ham to a medical van and put on his space suit. They placed Ham in his couch, securing him with zippers and laces, and attached his biosensors. Then, the sergeant plugged in Ham's levers and light panel.

Scientists planned two kinds of lever tests for Ham's mission:

Test 1: When a red light above Ham's right-hand lever came on, he had to press the lever at least once every fifteen seconds.

Test 2: Every two minutes, a blue light above Ham's left-hand lever would come on. He had five seconds to press the lever.

The tests would overlap, forcing Ham to follow the two different lights and their different timings *at the same time*.

Ham studied the sergeant's serious face.

Half an hour later, Sergeant Dittmer carried Ham to a transfer van, where engineers and technicians tested and retested Ham's biosensors, levers, and lights. Every five minutes, a veterinarian measured the chimp's vital signs. Everything looked good. Ham and the test panel were fit to fly!

Minnie moved to the medical van and went through the same prep steps. She would become the first astrochimp if anything went wrong with Ham.

At 3:02 AM, Ham and Minnie ate a small breakfast in their couches. When they finished, technicians secured their lids with tie-down bolts and attached the air hoses. Engineers checked both couches for air leaks while the astrochimps tested their consoles with 15 minutes of lever tests.

Two hours later, at T-minus 5 hours, 50 minutes, trainers drove Ham to the launchpad. Sergeant Dittmer carried Ham up the gantry and placed him in the spacecraft.

Ham waited, more than 80 feet in the air, staring at the Atlantic Ocean through his couch window.

Visions of Exploding Rockets

The destruct officer sat very still, his right pointer finger hovering over a red button. If Ham's rocket misbehaved, the officer would blow it up—immediately.

For years the air force had used its red-button policy to protect nearby residents and tourists. The debris would fall into the ocean if the officer hit the detonate button when the rocket first went off course, instead of onto people. But now the policy had a more important goal: preventing World War III. Cape Canaveral was just a few hundred miles from Cuba, an island country. Just six months ago, the Soviets declared they would protect Cuba with "rocket fire." If a spacecraft or its booster rocket exploded too high in the air, Cuba might mistake it for an American attack.

The sergeant's heart pounded. He and his team had worked toward this event for more than two years. Excitement competed with fear: "I had been down there [at Cape Canaveral] when some of their missiles had exploded over the ocean; you know—the missiles were off track and they just hit the [detonator] button on them. And I didn't want that to happen to Ham."

Sergeant Dittmer returned to get Minnie, then drove to a standby site near the launchpad. The sergeant's work was done. Like the rest of the world, all he could do now was watch and wait.

With the spacecraft's hatch still open, scientists gave Ham three more lever tests. Later, they would compare these baseline scores with Ham's flight scores during microgravity and strong g-forces.

At 7:10 AM, technicians closed the hatch. The three-year-old astrochimp waited in the tiny metal spacecraft, on an 83-foot-tall Redstone rocket, alone.

Fifty-five minutes later, technicians rolled the gantry away from the launchpad. The cherry picker waited in place, but it couldn't save Ham if there was a fire or fuel leak. NASA had not trained the astrochimps to escape from spacecrafts.

Mercury Seven astronauts Wally Schirra and Deke Slayton "flew chase" in fighter jets, circling the launch-pad at a safe distance. They listened to the official countdown through their cockpit radios. The other Mercury Seven astronauts waited offshore for liftoff on the deck of a navy destroyer ship, binoculars in hand.

Coast guard ships and air force planes kept a close eye on the Soviet "fishing boats" anchored off the Cape, hovering (just barely) in international waters. Large antennas on the boat decks revealed their true motives. NASA worried the Soviets could detonate a spacecraft's booster rocket from these boats.

The countdown continued. Engineers, technicians, veterinarians, and military brass tensed as the seconds passed. Ham's trainers stood in a small block house, close to the blast site.

Inside Mission Control, a red light suddenly blinked a warning: a glitch with the power adapter caused it to overheat. The countdown stopped.

Workers reopened Ham's spacecraft's hatch to cool the adapter. Did Ham think he'd finished another practice day?

An hour later, at 10:15 AM, technicians resealed Ham's spacecraft.

The countdown restarted at T-minus 2 hours. (Thankfully, NASA did not need to repeat some of the steps.) By now, Ham had waited in his couch for almost *eight* hours.

At T-minus 2 minutes, Ham started his lever tests.

Up, Up, and Away

At 11:54 AM, the final countdown began. This was it: the moment the United States could surge forward in the Space Race.

T-minus 10, 9, 8, 7, 6, 5, 4, 3, 2, 1, liftoff!

The rocket rested on a base of flames. Then it climbed and climbed, thundering into space, soon reaching 5,800 miles per hour. A vapor cloud chased the rocket, marking the route with a fluffy white line.

The Florida weather was just right: no rain and few clouds. From NASA staff to tourists, everyone at Cape Canaveral looked up, watching the Redstone rocket power America's first astronaut, an astrochimp, into the skies above.

Out in the Atlantic Ocean, a dozen navy ships waited for the astrochimp's splashdown. The winds and seas were calm. NASA expected a simple rescue and recovery.

For people watching the launch at the Cape or on television, the flight looked perfect. Mission Control—and Ham—knew otherwise. A faulty valve sent too much liquid oxygen into the rocket's fuel tank. The extra fuel sent Ham into space much faster than planned, causing a sudden 17 g of crushing force.

The skin around Ham's eyes stretched tight, like a rubber band about to snap. Muscles slammed against bones and blood vessels. His couch shook back and forth. Ham's pulse soared to 158 beats per minute, almost twice his liftoff rate.

A few minutes later, when the engine stopped firing, the astrochimp hit 0 g. For six and one-half minutes, Ham's body relaxed in microgravity. He took a break from his test questions, gazing out the window.

When his spacecraft rounded the flight's arc, the 0 *g* party ended. Reentry g-forces welcomed Ham to a new flight stage, slamming him back against his couch.

At Mission Control, a scary silence filled the room. Ham's radio signal had died.

Splashdown

Over the Atlantic Ocean, all eyes watched the sky.

Five navy spotter planes circled, waiting for Ham's spacecraft to fall through the clouds.

Twelve navy destroyer ships also waited, spaced 25 miles apart under Ham's flight path. Each ship carried at least one veterinarian and a vet tech. "We sat there waiting and listening and listening to radios," veterinarian Bill Britz remembers. "We thought maybe we had lost him."

The USS *Donner* waited in the center of the target zone, the place mathematicians predicted Ham would land. The *Donner* wasn't just any destroyer ship. It carried three helicopters from the 22nd Marine Helicopter Squadron. Veterinarians, doctors, and NASA officials sailed with the ship, eager to see whether space had affected the astrochimp.

Every ship wanted to rescue Ham, even the last one in line, a small ship called the USS *Ellison*.

Rough Landing

Ooouuccccchhhh! Ham's nose slammed against his test console, stinging. His screech echoed in the small couch.

The extra energy in the escape rocket's misfire sent Ham 42 miles higher than planned, increasing his landing force. And then a braking rocket failed.

The crash punched small holes in the spacecraft. Water rushed in.

A few minutes later, the landing bag started to shred. The spacecraft turned on its side.

Ham lay in his couch, bobbing in choppy waves, waiting.

Search planes filled the sky, looking left, right, up, down. Every moment mattered. Ham's couch had enough oxygen for just 24 hours.

Ham's spacecraft was nowhere near the landing spot predicted by NASA's math whizzes. The numbers were simple: liftoff force multiplied by the spacecraft's mass minus adjustments for the angle. The astrochimp should be right *here*, in the target zone.

The planes searched in wider and wider circles. Were they looking for something that wasn't there? If the parachutes failed, the spacecraft was probably on the ocean floor by now.

Finally! A plane spotted Ham! The extra energy in the escape rocket's misfire had sent his spacecraft 237 miles farther than planned, overshooting the target zone by more than 130 nautical miles. The rescue planes had been searching in the wrong place.

The copilot dropped a smoke bomb and green dye near the spacecraft to repel sharks and help the spacecraft stand out in the waves. The news quickly spread over plane and ship radios and on to NASA.

Ham had splashed down in the Caribbean, about 225 miles from the Bahamas. Even at top speed, Ham's rescue ship, the *Donner*, was six and a half hours away.

Ham landed closest to the *Ellison*, the rescue ship farthest from NASA's target zone. Excitement surged through the *Ellison*'s crew as their ship powered toward the astrochimp. They expected to be a few hundred miles from the Space Race action, and now they were right in the middle of it! They might even rescue the astronaut!

Three hours later, the *Ellison* reached Ham. Fear rippled through the crew. They could barely see the spacecraft. Floating on its side, the spacecraft was drowning in three- to four-foot waves.

The captain held back, stopping about 150 yards from the spacecraft. He didn't want the ship's wake to sink the spacecraft—and Ham.

The captain needed a new plan. Fast. He sent two crewmembers down a ladder on the edge of the ship and into a small rubber raft. These weren't just any crewmembers. They were skilled swimmers and divers called "frogs." Frantically, the frogs rowed toward the spacecraft, ropes in hand. If they could lasso Ham's spacecraft, they might get enough grip to pull it right side up.

Just as the frogs neared the spacecraft, a thundering tornado of wind lowered from the sky. A marine helicopter's large, powerful blades stirred up stronger waves, almost capsizing the frogs' small raft. Salty ocean mist burned the men's eyes as they rowed out of the helicopter's way.

Arcade Games in the Sky

The helicopter's door slid open. A marine leaned out the door on his belly. He lowered a steel cable down to the sea. The goal? To hook the cable to the top of Ham's spacecraft so the helicopter could lift it out of the ocean and fly Ham back to the larger, fully staffed ship, the *Donner*.

From the decks of the *Ellison*, the rescue attempts looked like the claw arcade game. The prize was right there, just like the most tempting plush toy in the claw's prize bin: all the helicopter had to do was grab it.

Back and forth the copter went, hovering over the spacecraft, searching for the hook.

The pilots had practiced these moves hundreds of times, but choppy ocean waves were much different than Florida's calm Banana River. And the rotor blades blew up a blinding seaspray. They couldn't even see the loop.

The helicopter powered up and circled around for another try.

The copilot stopped wasting time looking for the lifting loop. Instead, he lowered his 12-foot-long pole with its shepherd's hook beneath the water near the neck of the spacecraft, blindly searching.

After a few floundering minutes, the copilot hooked the loop. *Yes!*

The helicopter's pilot, Lieutenant John Hellriegel, shifted out of autopilot mode and started raising the spacecraft. "We've got it, but, boy, is this thing heavy," he reported over his radio.

Two more helicopters arrived on the scene, joining the first copter in loose formation. The *Ellison's* crew lined the deck in dismay as the spacecraft faded into the horizon.

Now the pilots' task was simple: fly Ham across the ocean to the *Donner* and lower his spacecraft onto the ship's deck. The *Donner* was about 90 miles away, heading toward them at top speed.

The pilots scanned the water ahead, searching for the ship. Shouldn't it already be here? Copilot Lieutenant Wayne Koons recalled the stress of the moment: "We were assuming the ship was at point so-and-so [and coming toward us]. . . . As we approached the point where we should be able to see the ship, which is normally about eight miles, there was no ship in view."

But the *Donner* wasn't close. Or even on its way. The navy's prize ship was dead in the water; it had lost all power when changing fuel tanks. A generator let crewmembers use their radios for a few minutes to talk with the helicopter pilots. But after that, they couldn't talk to planes, helicopters, or other ships.

Fear surged through the pilot and copilot. Ham's spacecraft had taken in water, so it weighed much more now than it had in training sessions. The extra weight burned more fuel. "At this point," said Lieutenant Koons, "all we could do was keep going."

About five miles from the ship, Lieutenants Koons and Hellriegel saw red. A warning light blinked on the instrument panel, announcing low fuel.

The copter pilots reported to the *Donner's* crew that they had "a very heavy spacecraft in a very low fuel state." The pilots sounded calm, but this was an emergency! If the helicopter ran out of fuel, it would crash onto the spacecraft and both vehicles would sink.

In hundreds of practice drills, the copter always lowered the spacecraft onto a stack of mattresses on the recovery ship's deck. The helicopter would stay nearby while crewmembers released the astrochimp. Then, the crew would move the spacecraft and the mattresses to clear landing space for the copter.

Since the helicopter had so little fuel, the pilots changed the plan. There was no time to hover above the ship. Instead, the crew needed to *move the spacecraft and the mattress immediately, before the copter crashed.* No one argued with the pilots.

At 3:40 PM, the helicopter placed Ham's spacecraft on the *Donner's* deck. The crew raced in to move the spacecraft, which now weighed more than 2,000 pounds, and then the mattress. Moments later, the copter landed. *Phew!*

Silence

Startled, hundreds of crewmembers stared at the spacecraft. The heat shield was gone, tattered straps dangling in its place.

Mission Control knew nothing. It lost radio contact with Ham's spacecraft during the last three minutes of his trip. Did 0 *g* affect Ham's heart? Did the harsh landing hurt him? Did the spacecraft overheat? *Was he even alive?*

A helicopter drops Ham's spacecraft on the *Donner*'s deck. Soon after, crewmembers rushed in to move the spacecraft and the mattress, making room for the copter's emergency landing. *NASA*

So much mattered at this moment. If the astrochimp survived space, NASA could schedule a human flight. If not, the United States would fall even further behind the Soviets.

Two minutes later, technicians removed the spacecraft's door hatch. A foot and a half of water rested just a few inches below the door, sloshing around Ham's couch.

Everyone leaned forward, trying to catch a glimpse inside the couch. The chimp's window had fogged over, clouding their view.

Slowly, through the background noise of a hundred muffled conversations, people near the spacecraft realized some of the sounds around them were coming from Ham. *Glorious chimp sounds!* A reporter on the ship described the noise as "a cross between a kitten's meow and a baby's cry." He was alive!

Technicians unhooked the couch's air supply system and started pumping oxygen into the astrochimp's couch. His cloudy window cleared.

Ham's nose stood out, bruised. He had vomited, perhaps from seasickness during three and a half hours of bobbing in choppy waves, sideways and upside down. Or maybe he gulped in too much air while struggling in rising water? Otherwise, he seemed OK.

Technicians reached into the spacecraft, struggling to unhook the couch. They had practiced this step a lot, but never with a spacecraft full of water. Working blind slowed them down.

As technicians toiled for the next 25 minutes, Ham cried. Veterinarian Richard Benson reassured the nervous faces around him: "He's talking to us."

Ham "turned his head from side to side, watching onlookers curiously and licking his pink chops. He reached a couple of fingers of his right hand through the air port to grasp the hand of Benson," said a reporter.

At last, technicians hoisted the astrochimp's couch out of the spacecraft and removed its cover.

There . . . was . . . Ham.

The Burp Heard Around the World

Ham crossed his arms in front of his chest. Then he burped. Loudly. An Associated Press reporter described the scene this way: "Ham looks serenely at the earthbound creatures, his face the picture of self-satisfaction."

Dr. Joseph Brady, the astrochimps' lead psychologist, reported it another way: "The hatch was opened on the flight deck and the chimp came out sputtering and thrashing about." A nearby admiral shook his head: "If that chimp could only talk." Oh, no, Dr. Brady responded. Thank goodness Ham *couldn't* talk, "or the space program might come to an abrupt end right on the spot."

Dr. Benson leaned over Ham to check the chimp's vital signs. Ham held Dr. Benson's left hand while the doctor worked. Ham knew Dr. Benson well, and the doctor's touch consoled him. When Dr. Benson finished the exam, he gave the astrochimp an apple and they shook hands.

Now it was time to pose. The *Donner's* captain stood behind Ham's couch. He leaned one arm around Ham's couch to shake the astrochimp's hand, smiling for the photographer. After the captain left, crew members came over for photos.

At first, the new people intrigued Ham. He studied their faces as they beamed for the camera. Some sailors shook Ham's hand without looking at him. Others touched just the tips of Ham's fingers with their arm extended, as though he were something icky they needed to hold from afar. Ham kept looking over his shoulder to watch the new people. Sometimes he stretched out his arms to them.

After a while, Ham stopped trying to connect with people. He was sleepy and his nose hurt. Instead, he pouted, gazing past the photographer, waiting for the strangers to leave.

During Ham's photoshoots, a *Donner* helicopter flew back to the *Ellison* to pick up some cameras. For the *Ellison's* crew, losing Ham's spacecraft to the *Donner* felt like losing the championship game in triple overtime. The ship's captain politely handed over the cameras. But as the copter lifted up, the kitchen crew took revenge, pelting the copter with potatoes and oranges as the whole ship cheered.

Back on board the *Donner*, technicians carried Ham to the ship's sick bay for more medical tests. The astrochimp spent the night with Dr. Benson in the ship's VIP suite, a place usually reserved for generals and dignitaries.

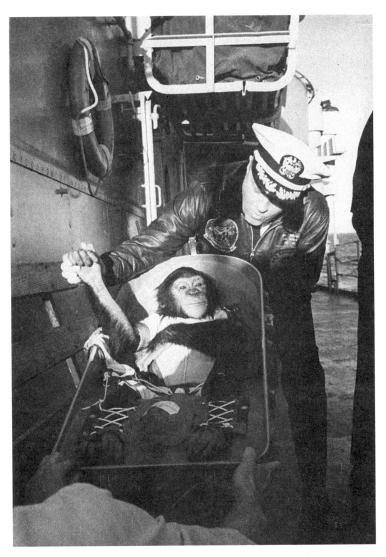

The captain of the USS *Donner* shakes hands with America's first astronaut. Ham's safe return provided engineers, technicians, and recovery crews with valuable details about suborbital space travel. *NASA*

The next day Ham got another helicopter ride. This time he rode *inside* the copter, instead of dangling from a cable beneath it. The helicopter landed on a hospital ship in the Grand Bahamas, so Ham could get more detailed medical exams. Had the strong g-forces damaged his eyes? Had 0 *g* changed his blood? Veterinarians and doctors would find out.

Lieutenant Colonel Betty Jo Wilson Canter, an army nurse, helped with the astrochimp's exams. When doctors asked her to hold Ham, she hesitated: "I didn't know if he was angry or what. He seemed nice. I took him and he put his arms around me like a little baby." When they finished, Ham flew back to the Cape.

Sergeant Dittmer paced the tarmac, waiting for Ham's plane. Ah, there it was, moving through the sky like any other plane on any other day. When the door opened, Ham jumped from the nurse's lap and flew down the stairs. "Boy," said the sergeant, "he ran right to me!" Ham jumped into the Sergeant Dittmer's arms, clinging to safety.

A Pentagon general expressed the relief many people felt: "I'm sure glad that little fellow made it. He's not like a man, you know. A man could have turned that assignment down."

Close Calls

While doctors and trainers studied Ham, engineers and scientists examined the astrochimp's spacecraft. What could they learn to help the human astronauts?

The air inside Ham's couch rose 7 degrees Fahrenheit during his flight, but the extra heat did not hurt him. Ham's couch vibrated more than usual, which may have scared him.

Ham leans into army nurse Betty Jo Wilson Canter after his postflight health exams. *NASA*

The couch vibrations could have killed Ham, said Frank Samonski, one of NASA's mechanical engineers. "The hoses were connected to that chimp couch the same way they were to the pressure suit, sort of a supply hose and a return hose. Well, during launch, this inlet snorkel [valve] vibrated open, and that allowed, through another valve, all the cabin air to escape. So the cabin depressurized. It's a pretty serious kind of thing. And if not for a little check valve that separated this pressure suit circuit from this [duct that ran] up to the snorkel valve, we'd have lost that chimpanzee."

The water leaks caused by the high-force landing could have been deadly too. Robert Thompson, an aeronautical engineer, confirmed the wisdom of the *Ellison* captain's decision not to create wake near the spacecraft: "It turns out, as we reconstructed and measured the water that was in the spacecraft, it was just about ready to sink."

Test Grades

Ham's space trip was much more than a joy ride. He worked during the trip, taking color and counting tests.

On his blue-light tests, Ham earned a perfect score. He had five seconds to press the lever, but he always did it in less than one. When scientists compared Ham's prelaunch scores on Earth to his scores in space, they were thrilled. He was two one-hundredths of a second slower in space!

During the first two minutes of his trip, Ham pressed his red-light lever more than 160 times—that's 1.3 times per second!

For the next 20 seconds, the unexpected force of 17 g slowed Ham down. He pressed a lever just seven times. "I find it amazing that Ham worked at all in so much extra g-force," says trainer Dr. Vernon Pegram.

In microgravity, the astrochimp returned to his quick lever speeds. At nine minutes into his trip, when reentry g-forces hit, his pace slowed again. Ham kept working at these slower speeds as parachutes opened and during and right after the spacecraft's high-force landing.

Ham missed just two test questions during his flight: one during the strong acceleration g-forces and the other right after landing.

Fred Matthews, an engineer with NASA's Space Task Group, described Ham's first mistake. When Ham reached the top of the flight arc, "a big flash of sunlight came in through the window. . . . We could tell what was happening because we had a time-lapse camera in there. Every second it was taking a picture of what was going on. That's how we could tell he was doing a perfect job, up until that moment. The flash of sunlight caught his attention. He looked out, looked down, saw the ocean down below and all the islands and so forth, and was fascinated." Then he missed a test question. It took years for NASA to learn this lesson from Ham: don't fill the flight plan with too many tasks. *Give the astronauts some time.*

Ham's trip answered NASA's big science question, proving that primate brains work in space. *Success!*

Fame and Glory

When Ham landed at the Cape, Sergeant Dittmer and the trainers were waiting for him. Dittmer carried Ham back to the other astrochimps, who greeted him with hugs and handshakes.

The next day, NASA arranged a news conference at the Cape. They planned to tell stories about the astrochimp's trip. Then they would bring Ham out for photos in a model spacecraft and couch. Almost 300 NASA employees, military staff, and more than two dozen reporters waited for the event to begin. Excitement swirled through the air.

Trainers dressed Ham in his space uniform. But a simple uniform wasn't enough today. NASA had custom-made a fancy outfit for their astrochimp: white pants, a black leather flight jacket with the Mercury spacecraft embroidered on the back, and high-top basketball shoes.

The press conference started well. Lieutenant Colonel James Henry, a NASA official in the life science division, announced the good news: "Our preliminary studies lead us to believe that, physiologically, a [human] astronaut would have been perfectly all right on this trip."

Now the reporters needed photos. Ham walked out, looking smart and oh-so-cute.

When Ham realized they planned to put him inside the couch, his muscles tensed. Screeching, screaming, and flashing his teeth in terror, Ham leaped into Sergeant Dittmer's arms, clinging to the sergeant's neck, *refusing* to get in the couch. Startled, the audience jumped back, scaring the astrochimp even more.

America's first astronaut, Ham, greets reporters in his uniform. His mission provided engineers, technicians, and recovery crews with valuable suborbital space experience. *NASA*

Veterinarians rushed Ham and the sergeant indoors. A trainer slid one of his fingers inside Ham's cheek. Gently, Ham chewed on the finger, slowly calming down. Dr. Pegram watched the scene, shaking his head. "I certainly didn't blame him," he says.

Reporters shuffled back and forth: deadlines called. A drizzling rain dampened their notepads.

An hour later, the vets brought the astrochimp out again. At first, Ham acted the same. More screeching! More clinging! The people-pleasing chimp had his limits.

After a few minutes, Ham relaxed, entertaining the crowd by playing patty-cake with a trainer. No one dared bring him back to the spacecraft. Alan Shepard often joked about this day. "The only reason that I got to fly," he'd say, "was because Ham refused to get back in the spacecraft."

In the morning, Sergeant Dittmer met Ham in the classroom and set up more tests. The sergeant knelt beside Ham, guiding him into the work chair with a calming voice.

Ham did two 30-minute tests that day and another test the next day. Why so many tests so soon? Hadn't Ham earned a vacation? Scientists needed to know whether space had changed the astrochimp's brain. To find out, they compared data from these new tests to his preflight data. The results made NASA happy: space travel had not changed Ham's test scores and reflex speeds. Thank goodness!

On February 4, 1961, Ham and the other five astro-chimps flew back to Holloman Air Force Base in New Mexico. NASA videotaped Ham's reunion. When he entered the chimp quarters, Ham moved to the farthest corner right away. The other chimps joined him, hugging and chatting.

Chipper Chimp?

Newspapers and magazines around the world loved Ham. They called him High-Flying Ham and Champ Chimp. They did not mention the astrochimp's response to his couch and spacecraft during the press conference.

Ham's trip meant progress for the United States. "Chipper Chimp Gives Go-Ahead for Space Man," declared the *Ottawa Journal*. "Chimp Trip Prelude for Spacemen," announced the Pennsylvania *Evening Standard*.

The Soviets paid close attention to Ham's trip. One Australian newspaper reported that "the Soviet press and radio last night gave unusual prominence to the United States' chimpanzee space flight. . . . During the past year, US space achievements have been completely ignored, although failures have been widely publicized."

A week later, NASA shared photos taken inside the astrochimp's spacecraft. Ham's humanlike emotions startled people. Curiosity. Anger. Fear. He didn't look like a silly circus animal enjoying a roller coaster ride. And he certainly wasn't "chipper" during 17 g! People who studied wild chimps, such as Dr. Jane Goodall, instantly knew the truth: Ham's open-mouthed grin showed terror, not joy.

The following Associated Press article ran in newspapers across the country. Images from the spacecraft's time-lapse camera changed the story.

ROCKET RIDE FILM SHOWS HAM IN HAM

WASHINGTON, February 9, AP — Ham the chimpanzee lived up to his name, hamming it up for all he was worth in a motion picture of his recent rocket ride into space.

His grimaces, flashing eyes and toothy scowls outdid some of the most flamboyant stars of the silent movie days as he portrayed the role of the intrepid explorer venturing into the unknown. . . .

The picture was all in close-ups and the rubber-faced little ape made the most of it. His wild-eyed glances over his shoulder as the Redstone rocket shot him along at [more than] 5,000 miles per hour were more expressive than those of any terrified maiden fleeing from a Hollywood villain.

And no actor has ever shown angry frustration more clearly than Ham did when a booster rocket suddenly slammed him back against his couch with 17 times the force of gravity. He bared his teeth with the ferocity of Boris Karloff [an English actor famous for his horror movies] but his eyes remained pure Charlie Chaplin.

Moving Closer

Ham's flight fueled America's frenzy to get a human into space before the Soviets. Space science seemed certain now. If an astrochimp could breathe and think in microgravity, a human astronaut could too. Human blood wouldn't boil. Human eyeballs wouldn't pop out. *Thank you, Ham!*

Soon, NASA announced that Alan Shepard would make the first human suborbital space trip. A navy pilot who had tested the Demon, Crusader, Skyray, and

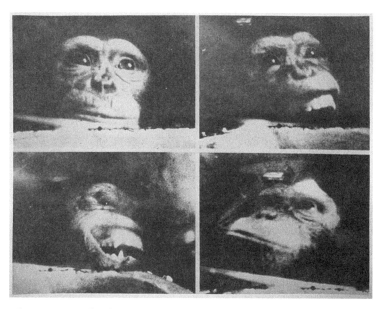

Chimpanzee biologists instantly knew the truth when they saw photos from Ham's 16-minute flight. His open-mouthed grin showed fear, not joy. The chimp and human astronauts had not trained for so much g-force. *NASA*

Tigercat airplanes, Colonel Shepard became NASA's new star. Like the other Mercury Seven astronauts, Alan Shepard despised NASA's slow, cautious pace. And he really disliked those astrochimps. Ham stole *his* flight.

"The irony of playing second fiddle to a chimpanzee was particularly galling to us," explained Shepard. "NASA had decided to send a chimp into space before sending me. I protested again and again, but NASA insisted the little ape go first. The agency meant well. But all I could think about were Russian boosters rolling to their pads for the first manned spaceflight."

Once, recalled Sergeant Dittmer, when someone asked Colonel Shepard why NASA chose him as America's first astronaut, Shepard said, "I guess they ran out of monkeys!" Alan Shepard was no dummy. He had an engineering degree from the US Naval Academy. He knew Ham was an ape—he used the word *monkey* as an insult.

After Ham's trip, the Mercury Seven became the butt of astrochimp jokes. A famous cartoon showed Ham in a classroom teaching space science to the human astronauts, promising them bananas if they pushed the right buttons. In another cartoon, Ham told Alan Shepard that he would crave a banana during his flight.

NASA workers also teased the astronauts. "We would joke about how our chimps trained men to go into outer space," admitted Howard Blackburn, an astrochimp trainer. Some people dared to tease Colonel Shepard to his face.

One day, Alan Shepard climbed into the transport van for a practice run to the launchpad. A jokester had taped a sketch of a suborbital flight path in front of Shepard's seat. The Mercury Seven knew these drawings by heart. But this one looked different. Someone had plotted Ham's higher and longer trip *over* Alan Shepard's path. The colonel's face burned red.

Try as they might, the human astronauts could not ignore the astrochimps.

Timing Is Everything

If America wanted the title of First Human in Space, NASA had to act quickly. The Soviets knew about Ham's flight from television reports and spy boats. Their engineers and cosmonauts worked fast and furious.

But America's pace lagged. Moving slowly and steadily, NASA's engineers worried that their space technology was not ready for human travel. The environmental control systems needed more work, and Ham's painful splashdown had told NASA their new landing bag still wasn't strong enough. Engineers put a spacecraft and a landing bag in a water tank. They "hit it with waves for about 20 minutes, and it just tore all to pieces," said Robert Thompson, a NASA engineer.

Engineers began testing new landing-bag designs, adding steel cables and an extra support bar at the bottom of the spacecraft. They also designed a hatch door for emergencies. When Ham almost sank, NASA realized the astronauts needed a way to escape if rescue planes and helicopters couldn't find the spacecraft right away.

Doctors from the National Academy of Sciences still worried. They wanted *six* chimpanzee flights before a human went to space. At least one NASA doctor still thought space travel could hurt humans. He argued NASA should run 50 chimps through intense centrifuge training before flying a human. Fifty chimpanzees sounded tame compared to President Kennedy's Science Advisory Committee: it wanted to test 100 chimps on centrifuges.

The Science Advisory Committee also wanted more astrochimp missions. A dead astronaut would hurt the space program—and the president. Some committee members wanted to fly *two dozen or more* chimps before flying a human.

But more astrochimp trips were not a perfect solution. Dr. Robert Voas, a navy psychologist who worked with astronauts on NASA's Space Task Group, described the "public relations problem" of using chimpanzees as stand-ins for humans. The public adored the astrochimps. They were America's astronauts, just like the Mercury Seven men. "It turned out that you had to be very careful, because the press was following the program so closely that if one of your animals died, the issue would be 'Wouldn't the astronaut be dead?'"

The Mercury Seven astronauts didn't care what doctors or politicians thought. *Now. We need to go NOW* echoed through every conversation. Alan Shepard even shared this view with President Kennedy at a White House party. President Kennedy knew Alan Shepard's comment broke the chain of command. The president asked Colonel Shepard what NASA's director, James Webb, thought about fast-tracking a human flight. Yes, Alan Shepard admitted, the director wanted one more unmanned trip to fix Ham's liftoff problems and fine-tune the ECS.

On April 12, the debates ended. The Soviets announced that cosmonaut Yuri Gagarin had traveled to space. The Soviet Union had won the race to get a human in space.

Americans sighed in grief. For the Mercury Seven astronauts, their disappointment ached like a gut punch. If only NASA had sent Alan Shepard to space instead of astrochimp Ham.

The bad news kept coming. Yuri Gagarin had not just nipped the edge of space in an arc, as Ham had. Instead, the cosmonaut had flown *around* Earth in an *orbital* flight—a much more complex feat than Ham's flight.

Two days later, NASA tested the powerful Atlas rocket. Could it get America in orbit? A few seconds after liftoff, the rocket collapsed back onto the launchpad.

One good thing came from Yuri Gagarin's trip, though. "When Yuri Gagarin flew and he got back all right, it sort of negated the [pressure for] six [chimpanzee] flights," said Max Faget, NASA's lead engineer.

Although Ham's trip was *sub*orbital and Yuri Gagarin's was *orbital*, the space travelers had a lot in common. One of Gagarin's booster engines stayed on about one-half of a second too long. The extra force propelled Gagarin almost 60 miles higher into orbit than planned, causing fiercer g-forces, just like Ham had faced.

Also like Ham, the extra force from Gagarin's rocket sent him more than 100 miles away from his target recovery zone. Instead of using retro-rockets to slow down for landings, Soviet cosmonauts left by parachute, a few thousand feet before their spacecrafts crashed. When Yuri Gagarin parachuted from his spacecraft, he landed in a freshly plowed field, surprising a local woman and her five-year-old granddaughter who were planting potatoes. Too bad Ham and Gagarin couldn't chat about space travel over coffee and banana bread.

Puppy Politics

President John Kennedy and Premier Nikita Khrushchev in the Soviet Union exchanged letters and gifts, despite fighting a Cold War and a Space Race. Maybe they liked each other. Or maybe they wanted to keep their enemy close.

Less than a month after Yuri Gagarin's flight, the two leaders met for a summit in Vienna, Austria. At a state dinner, Mrs. Kennedy asked Premier Khrushchev about Strelka's puppies.

Strelka was a sensitive subject with President Kennedy. In August 1960 Strelka and another mixed-breed dog made 18 orbits around Earth. She reminded the president that the Soviets were far ahead.

A few months later, one of Strelka's puppies, Pushinka, arrived at the White House. Surprise! Pushinka means *fluffy* in Russian, and she was, indeed, very fluffy. This barking symbol of the Soviet space program angered President Kennedy. But he kept that feeling to himself when he wrote a thank-you note to Chairman Khrushchev.

The president's letter said he and Mrs. Kennedy were "particularly pleased to receive Pushinka. Her flight from the Soviet Union to the United States was not as dramatic as the flight of her mother, nevertheless it was a long voyage and she stood it well." President Kennedy did not mention that army intelligence officers had x-rayed Pushinka, searching for spy devices!

When Pushinka had puppies with Charlie, another family dog, the president called them *pupniks,* after the Sputnik satellites.

No Diapers on Board

Three months later, it was Alan Shepard's turn. Finally. Like America, Colonel Shepard had run out of patience. He'd been ready to fly for so long. And while he waited, a freckle-faced chimpanzee stole his glory. Then Yuri Gagarin claimed the First Human in Space title. *Ouch.*

Colonel Shepard sat on top of a Redstone rocket, strapped into a cramped spacecraft, just like Ham. The night before, Colonel Shepard joked about the astrochimp with a friend: "Maybe [NASA] should make this chimpanzee routine complete and bring Ham down here to observe my blastoff."

Pushinka enjoys the treehouse slide at the White House play-ground. Pushinka's mom, Strelka, orbited Earth in a Soviet spacecraft more than a year before America launched astro-chimp Ham into space. *Cecil Stoughton, White House Photographs, John F. Kennedy Presidential Library and Museum*

Four. Long. Hours. Passed.

Astronauts Wally Schirra and Scott Carpenter watched from above, flying their jets in wide, slow circles around the launchpad.

Pad Leader Guenter Wendt huddled nearby with his emergency crew. "Visions of exploding rockets kept running through my head, and the wait seemed to be endless," Wendt said.

Technical problems and thunderstorms kept stopping the countdown. A flustered Colonel Shepard waited as engineers and technicians slowly reported their stations as GO or NO GO. After this flight, he would be famous. His face would cover more magazines and newspapers than that stinky chimpanzee. He would get awards and parades . . . *if* his rocket didn't explode . . . *if* his capsule didn't sink.

Each second felt like forever.

Hunger pains pinched the colonel's stomach. He'd burned through his breakfast long ago.

But hunger wasn't Colonel Shepard's only problem. Mercury spacecrafts were too small for bathrooms. Ham wore a diaper, but NASA assumed the human astronauts could *just hold it*. After hours of countdown delays, Alan Shepard couldn't wait any more. He tried. He *really* tried. But he could hardly think about anything else.

Desperate, Colonel Shepard explained his problem to Gordon Cooper, the friend and fellow astronaut serving as the capsule communicator (CapCom). During long training sessions, the astronauts often peed in their space suits. Gross? Yes, but it took so long to get space suits off and on for bathroom breaks. If he peed in his space suit now, he could concentrate again.

Cooper talked with his bosses, who spoke with the medical team. Shepard didn't like their answer. No, he could not pee in his suit. Doctors feared the colonel's urine would short out the biosensors on his chest or signal his space suit to release cooling Freon gas.

Colonel Shepard couldn't take it anymore. *"Gordoooooo . . ."* he pleaded, "my bladder's gonna burst!"

The doctors huddled and brainstormed. Then they surrendered, disconnecting the power to Shepard's biosensors. Cooper gave him the OK over the radio: "Do it in the suit."

Ahhhh . . . Now the colonel was ready for space. Annoyed with the delays, he told mission controllers to "fix your little problem and light this candle."

At 9:34 AM, Alan Shepard blasted off in a mechanically perfect flight.

Colonel Shephard faced just 6.3 *g* getting into space, easy-peasy compared to Ham's 17 *g*.

At the top of the trajectory arch, Alan Shepard did the same thing as Ham: he stared out the window. Fascinated by the islands and ocean, the colonel ignored his tasks for a minute.

Fifteen minutes later, Colonel Shepard splashed down in the target zone. *Perfect!* Thanks to Ham's flight, Colonel Shepard's heat shield and landing bag worked like a charm.

The colonel flipped the rescue switch, releasing green dye and extending an antenna to help searchers find him. "At this point I could look out the left window and tell the dye marker package was working properly. The right window was still under water. I began looking around for . . . water inside but did not find any."

As his spacecraft bobbed in the water, Alan Shepard "kept thinking about the chimp's near disappearance beneath the ocean." He checked and rechecked the cabin for leaks.

Soon, Colonel Shepard heard from his rescue helicopter. He blew open the door hatch and sat in the doorway, waiting for his ride.

The copter hovered overhead. Slowly, it lowered a cable, then lifted the astronaut up and onboard.

As they flew across the ocean to the rescue ship, Lieutenant Wayne Koons, the pilot, and Lieutenant George Cox, the copilot, studied Alan Shepard. "We had been given some warnings by [one of] the astronauts' flight surgeons," explained Lieutenant Koons. "Now, you've got to keep an eye on him," the surgeon had warned. Since this was the first time a US astronaut had been weightless in space, they didn't know if Shepard would be "in his normal state of mind."

Compared to a Chimp

After thousands of training hours, the Mercury Seven astronauts understood each detail of their missions. They knew when strong g-forces would hit. They knew the spacecrafts' antennae would guide recovery teams to them and that if their spacecrafts sank, scuba divers would search for them. The human astronauts carried shark repellant, extra food, a bright orange life raft, matches, and whistles, in case they had to eject. NASA doctors fitted the spacecrafts with medical kits, filled with painkillers, stimulants, and a drug to counter shock. In this case, knowledge helped.

On the other hand, the human astronauts knew about NASA's exploding rockets. They also knew that even the smallest math mistake could cause them to run out of fuel or get lost in space. The astrochimps didn't have that knowledge, so they didn't worry about those things.

Colonel Shepard's flight was a big deal for the United States, but the public kept comparing him to Ham. The astrochimp flew higher, farther, and longer *and* endured stronger g-forces than Alan Shepard. Ham also spent more time weightless in 0 *g*.

NASA's doctors compared the astronauts too. They embarrassed Colonel Shepard when they answered a reporter's question about surviving space: "You don't have to be a superman to go to space," one doctor said. "You'd probably black out, but you'd survive."

So doctors didn't respect his skills? And people compared him to a chimpanzee? Colonel Shepard fumed. If NASA hadn't used chimps as stand-ins for human astronauts, he would have been the first human in space. "That little race between Gagarin and me," he lamented over and over, "was really, really close."

Helicopter recovery of Mercury Seven astronaut Alan Shepard and his spacecraft. Instead of waiting inside the spacecraft, as Ham did, Shepard crawled through the escape hatch after splashdown, and rode back to the recovery ship inside the copter. *NASA*

Three weeks later, President Kennedy spoke to Congress about funding the space program, calling it one of the country's most "urgent national needs." The president asked Congress for $7 billion to $9 billion to fund "landing a man on the Moon and returning him safely to the Earth."

The president also surprised people by meeting with NASA's Space Task Group. Robert Gilruth, director of the group, said: "This was really the first time anyone of that high a level had expressed interest in manned space flight. . . . He had us all sit around with him in sort of a circle around his rocking chair. And he said, 'Tell me about space and your reactions to it.' Of course, everyone was just a little bit shy about expounding on how much he knew about space in that kind of company, so the President did most of the talking."

Back to Suborbital Space

A few months after Alan Shepard's trip, NASA sent Captain Gus Grissom on America's second suborbital trip. Things went well until splashdown, when Captain Grissom had to jump into the ocean before the rescue helicopter arrived.

Unfortunately, Captain Grissom left the oxygen intake valve in his space suit open. As his space suit lost air, it stopped floating. And as the suit filled with water, it started tugging the astronaut underwater.

Finally! The rescue copter arrived! Captain Grissom waved, pleading for help. The pilot and copilot didn't realize the astronaut was drowning—they thought he was waving hello!

Captain Grissom seemed OK, so the pilots turned to the sinking spacecraft. The helicopter's belly rested on the water, its front wheel underwater.

Frantically, the copilot reached underwater, searching for the spacecraft with a hook. *Phew,* found it!

The pilot tried to lift the waterlogged spacecraft, but the helicopter refused. Red warning lights flashed across the dashboard. The engine squealed, shredding steel. The copilot released the hook and watched the spacecraft fall back into the sea.

A second helicopter swept in to pick up Gus Grissom. *Whoa.* That was way too close. As they flew to safety, Captain Grissom's spacecraft sank to the ocean floor. Congress complained about the lost money, and the Soviets mocked yet another American failure. But at least the astronaut lived.

At first, NASA wanted all seven human astronauts to make suborbital flights before starting orbital missions. But the Soviet space victories ramped up the pressure to move America into deeper space. Since the astronauts looked healthy, NASA decided to stop making suborbital space trips.

NASA turned its attention to America's next space hurdle: catching up to the Soviets with *orbital* spaceflights. It was time for another chimpanzee trip.

RACING TO
DEEPER SPACE

To catch up with the Soviets in orbital space, NASA planned to test its new technology with at least one empty flight and one astrochimp flight.

Technically, an orbital trip is much different from a suborbital trip. To get a spacecraft into orbit requires a lot more energy than for a short suborbital trip, which doesn't go as high or as fast. An orbiting spacecraft would travel 17,500 miles per hour—or about five miles per second. That's more than three times faster than Ham's suborbital speed.

Faster speeds would cause more heat issues during reentry. NASA engineers invented a stronger heat shield to protect spacecrafts—and the astronauts inside them— from 2,000 fiery degrees Fahrenheit of heat. The new design would "absorb the growing heat until layers of it burned away. As these layers were vaporized and blown off, they would carry the heat away with them," explained Mercury Pad Leader Guenter Wendt. Pretty smart, huh?

NASA chose the Atlas rocket for its orbital flights. Five times more powerful than the Redstone rocket, the Atlas generated 360,000 pounds of thrust at liftoff. All that thrust made the Atlas a fuel hog, burning 2,000 pounds of fuel *per second*. Three engines powered the rocket: an inner sustainer engine and two outboard booster engines. The outboard engines fell off two minutes into the trip.

Despite its power, the Atlas rocket was pretty "flimsy," said Guenter Wendt. "Its skin was so thin that it could not support itself and its payload unless it was pressurized. Like a balloon full of air, the gas pressure gave it rigidity." This gas pressure made the Atlas rocket more dangerous than Ham's Redstone rocket. The Atlas was prone to tipping over, and even the smallest spark of static electricity could cause an explosion.

To improve liftoff safety, NASA replaced the cherry picker with a new rescue plan. If an Atlas exploded on the launchpad, a small escape tower rocket would shoot the spacecraft away from the flames. Then, the escape rocket's parachutes would float the astronaut back to land, far away from fire and fumes.

NASA engineers also struggled to lighten the spacecraft. Less weight would give the rocket more power to push the spacecraft into orbit.

NASA had to deal with other differences between suborbital and orbital flights. Astronaut John Glenn explained one big challenge in an interview with science writer Robert Stevens: "The cutoff speed and angle of the booster do not have to be extremely accurate [in suborbital flights]. But going into orbit, the craft must hit an exact spot at a certain speed and angle, with a precise power cutoff. Otherwise, it will not go into orbit, or it may go into the wrong orbit. After cutoff, the craft keeps a balance between gravity and centrifugal force."

To keep spacecrafts in Earth's orbit, NASA also needed tracking stations to communicate with Cape Canaveral's Mission Control—and with the astronaut—and with other tracking stations. Sound complicated? It was! NASA chose places around the world under the flight path.

Some tracking sites were so remote that it took more than two years to build the stations. NASA built on three continents and five islands, including sites in Eglin, Texas; White Sands, New Mexico; Point Arguello, California; Guaymas, Mexico; Kōke'e Park, Hawai'i; Tebaronga, Kanton Island; Woomera, Australia; Muchea, Australia; Stone Town, Zanzibar; Kano, Nigeria; Montana Blanca, Grand Canary Island; and Cooper's Island, Bermuda. Navy ships would serve as floating stations in the Indian and Pacific oceans.

Before NASA launched a spacecraft, each tracking station would have to report itself in GO condition. Each station had a large world map on a video screen. During the countdown, green circles marked stations in GO status. Orange circles showed stations with holds. And red circles labeled stations with big problems.

As an astronaut flew into each tracking center's range, a blinking green light around a spacecraft icon marked the path. The light would change to red when the spacecraft left a station's range. Astronaut Alan Shepard described the system this way: "The stations pass [the spacecraft] on from one to the other, like a baton in a relay race. Their radar devices 'acquire' it first, then lock

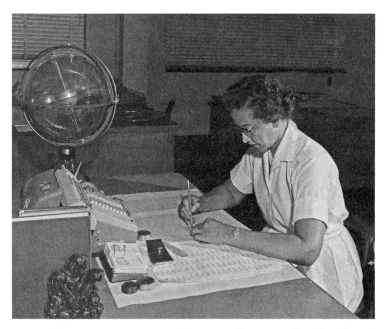

NASA human computer Katherine Johnson, who developed the trajectory math for America's suborbital and orbital astrochimp flights. NASA used same math for the human spaceflights. *NASA, Langley Research Center*

onto it and follow it until it leaves their area and heads for the next station."

To prevent confusion, the astronaut would talk to just one person on the ground: the capsule communicator (CapCom). NASA decided the Mercury Seven would serve as CapComs at some stations. It would help the astronauts learn more about orbital flights and bond them more as a team.

Bringing an orbital spacecraft back from space would require more speed and angle changes at just the right time. (The book and movie *Hidden Figures* highlighted the challenges involved in this GO / NO GO trajectory math.)

And then there were new problems. Speed demon Chuck Yeager had called the human astronauts *passengers* once too often. Now the Mercury Seven wanted NASA to redesign the spacecraft so they could be *pilots*.

NASA's engineers were on a deadline, with too much work and too little time. And now the human astronauts wanted *more* changes? Oh yes, they sure did.

Engineers added more than 100 control switches to do things such as fire retro-rockets and open parachutes. Astronauts could also steer their spacecrafts, using stars and the horizon as guides.

For America, these new technologies still needed testing, retesting, and more testing.

Pride and Propaganda

The Soviets had already mastered orbital spaceflight and eagerly planned ways to build on their success. They flaunted their plans too. Soviet premier Nikita Khrushchev praised cosmonaut Gagarin: "You have made yourself immortal because you are the first man to penetrate space."

The Central Intelligence Agency read each Soviet news story. For "four days," reported the CIA, "more than 90 percent of the monitored Soviet radio broadcasts were devoted to the event, covering such themes as 'Soviet superiority; Gagarin, the hero; world-wide acclaim; [and] peace and power.'"

The Soviet cosmonauts traveled to 28 countries, meeting fans and giving speeches. They taunted the United States: "We will not have to wait long" to get to the Moon.

On August 6, 1961, the Soviets announced a new victory. The Soviet cosmonaut Major Gherman Titov had orbited Earth 17 times on a 25-hour mission. In a spectacular version of "Look Mom, no hands," cosmonaut Titov turned off his radio for seven-and-a-half hours to sleep in peace.

America's space workers tried to ignore the Soviets. Instead, they focused on a new goal, testing the Atlas rocket. Scientists filled the Atlas-1 spacecraft with cameras, sound recorders, and equipment to measure heat, air pressure, and more. The trip would tell engineers and doctors whether an astrochimp could survive an orbital flight or whether they needed to make more changes.

The Atlas-1 countdown rippled through the national news. The entire world was watching. The engines fired, powering the rocket off the launchpad. People didn't realize they were holding their breath until they exhaled in unison. There she went . . . up . . . up . . . up.

And then, a minute later—*BOOOOOM!*

The explosion's force scattered debris across the Cape and nearby beaches. NASA collected the pieces so engineers could rebuild the rocket like a giant puzzle, searching for clues about what went wrong.

The world had watched America fail—again. But the world never saw the Soviets flounder. The Soviets didn't announce their space plans in advance, so their errors and explosions stayed secret. Americans wanted someone to blame. The country's largest space journal, *Missiles and Rockets*, targeted NASA: the "Mercury manned satellite program appears to be plummeting the United States toward a new humiliating disaster in the East-West space race."

Everyday people criticized NASA, writing heated letters to state senators and President Kennedy.

NASA received complaint letters, too. Some people didn't like the million-dollar budgets. Others were mad that the United States lagged so far behind the Soviets. A few people didn't want animals used as astronauts. Others argued it was "inhuman" to launch a person into space without proof it was safe. One official said, "Some letter writers to NASA say it is a shame to risk highly trained pilots. . . . We have been told to use convicts—on a volunteer basis. . . . But we have to use trained personnel. This is a scientific undertaking."

In the frenzy to win, people forgot some facts. Mercury-Atlas 1 exploded near the launchpad. The Mercury-Atlas 2 mission went well, but it was just a short suborbital test. Then the Mercury-Atlas 3 misbehaved soon after launch. Instead of arching sideways, it went straight up. NASA's destruct officer squeezed the red detonate button.

"The destruction of the Mercury-Atlas 3 left us dazed and disheartened," wrote Flight Director Gene Kranz in his autobiography *Failure Is Not an Option*. "After three successful suborbital missions, the jinx seemed broken; the odds were turning in our favor. Then the Atlas [3] had to be blown up."

To Chimp or Not to Chimp

Before America could beat the Soviets to the Moon, they had to get human astronauts into Earth's orbit. And before they did that, NASA needed an astrochimp to test-drive the technology.

NASA's leader, James Webb, warned overeager Americans: "If we are to have our spectacular successes . . . with even larger and ever more complex rockets, the early test flights, unmanned, of course, will involve spectacular failures."

But America had lost patience with failures and delays. If NASA skipped the astrochimp trip, the United States could surpass the Soviets. Soon, a five-way battle circled the astrochimps. Astronauts, politicians, engineers, physicians, and everyday people had opinions.

The Mercury Seven astronauts campaigned to skip the chimp trip. They were well trained and ready to go. It still hurt that the Soviets beat them to space by twenty-three days. Ham's First-American-in-Space title didn't help. The last thing the astronauts wanted was another chimpanzee stealing their thunder.

Was NASA too cautious? Or did it need an astro-chimp to test-drive its rockets and space math? The answer depended on whom you asked. The engineers wanted technical details, while doctors and psychologists needed medical information.

Five weeks after the Soviet's seventeen-orbit trip, NASA launched Mercury-Atlas 4 on a one-orbit trip around Earth. The flight had a mechanical astronaut on board, instead of a chimp or a human. For engineers, the "canned man" was "really much better than a live animal," said Max Faget. The pressurized box turned oxygen and carbon into CO_2 and water, and released heat, just like humans and chimps do when breathing. The canned man also collected data.

Demands to cancel the astrochimp flight spiked like a fever. People implored NASA to launch John Glenn instead. Hadn't the Mercury-Atlas 4 mission proven America ready? The rocket didn't explode at liftoff. The spacecraft circled Earth and returned home, as planned. What else could NASA want?

Chief of the Mercury medical team, Lieutenant Colonel Stanley White, disagreed, arguing it would be "extremely hazardous" to skip the chimpanzee flight.

"The MA-5 mission is more than a matter of just check-ing the spacecraft," he reminded everyone. Simply, doc-tors and psychologists did not know how orbital space would affect humans.

Would astrochimp Glenda be America's first female astro-naut? Pilot Jerrie Cobb offered to switch places with the chimp. *NASA*

Jerrie Cobb, who did astronaut tryout tests two years before with 12 other female pilots, did not like NASA's decisions either. When Cobb heard that astrochimp Glenda might get an orbital flight, she lost her cool. Had a chimpanzee stolen her chance to go to space? She told Congress that NASA respected female chimps more than women. Cobb even offered to switch places with Glenda! NASA said no—again.

Despite intense public pressure, NASA's doctors and engineers wanted an astrochimp to test the ECS and the Atlas rocket. Without the astrochimps, America's space dreams would stay on the ground.

The Right Chimp for the Job

The astrochimps didn't care about the debates swirling around them. They were busy.

Orbital flight training was harder than suborbital training. The chimps spent more time in the Vomit Comet and learned more color, shape, and counting skills. Ham still dazzled his trainers with his lever speeds and test scores, and he hadn't shrieked at a spacecraft since his press conference.

Trainers still used banana treats to reward the astrochimps. The chimps liked variety, though, so trainers made new flavors: orange, coconut, and maple-walnut. Astrochimp Bobby Joe had a better idea. Like wild chimps, Bobby Joe expected his friends to share. Why should he work for dried treats when he could pull his trainer toward a refrigerator filled with fresh fruits instead?

In late October, NASA gathered their new astro-chimp team at Cape Canaveral. The younger chimps, Rocky, Jim, and Ham, still had their fluffy white tail poofs. Enos and Duane were a little older. Every day, the chimps trained in mock spacecrafts at Hangar S, taking tests on colors, shapes, and counting. They made practice runs to the launchpad and flew on fighter jets to get used to louder engine noises.

Newspapers buzzed about Ham, America's favorite space star, as the launch date came closer. "Ham, the chimpanzee who blazed the space trail for America's first astronauts, is in the running for another rocket ride, but a fellow chimp has the edge right now," said one article. "Sources report one of the chimps, name not revealed, presently is doing a better job at learning his space tasks than Ham."

Two days before liftoff, NASA revealed the top astro-chimp: Enos. *Really?* The chimp who broke off a steel lever on his first day of space school would be America's first astronaut in orbital space?

During prelaunch checkups, Ham, Rocky, and Enos were "all in good health and close in the running," said Dr. Fineg, who chose the flight order with the lead psy-chologist. "I gave Enos the nod because he was the oldest, and because of his calmness and capacity to endure the stresses of the vigorous training program he had gone through." Rocky would serve as runner-up. Ham fell to number three. America's first astronaut still had good test scores, but he seemed less eager to please humans.

NASA did not choose Enos for his good looks or charm. His intelligence and work record set him apart from the competition. Enos had trained more than 1,200 hours in New Mexico and Kentucky. He exceled during

Enos drinks from a cup at a kitchen table. Note the cautious look on his handler's face! *NASA*

centrifuge training at the University of Southern California too. Simply put, Enos was the best astrochimp for the job.

Enos's résumé also included something unique. A month earlier, Enos underwent an experiment to measure the effects of long-term space travel. Instead of a few hours or days, this experiment ran for *two weeks*. For nine hours a day, Enos did lever tests inside a mock spacecraft. Some of these tests were harder than Ham's tests. It took the astrochimp about an hour to finish round 1. Then the questions started over again.

For 14 days, the only food and water Enos got were rewards for correct answers. During breaks, Enos stayed in the chair, alone. Scientists were impressed with the results. Enos lived on just the food and water he earned.

Even more amazing, Enos improved over time. In shape tests, Enos got 55 percent of the questions right on the first day. His scores kept going up. By day 13, he got 76 percent of the questions right. *Fast learner!*

NASA gave the astrochimp a good report: "Of the many factors which may affect both the behavior and physiology of a living organism during space flight, two of the most critical are restraint and social isolation. Certainly this is true when the organism is an active and gregarious chimpanzee. In fact, there was considerable doubt concerning the ability to restrain a chimpanzee for 14 days. But the results of this investigation prove conclusively that this is possible."

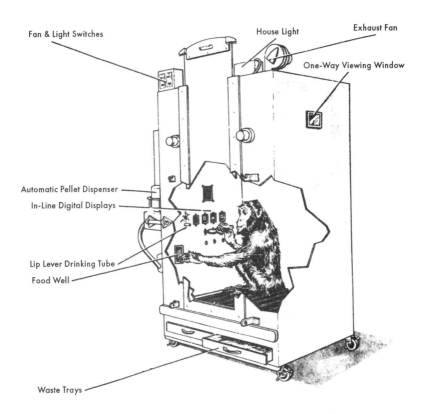

Fan & Light Switches · House Light · Exhaust Fan · One-Way Viewing Window · Automatic Pellet Dispenser · In-Line Digital Displays · Lip Lever Drinking Tube · Food Well · Waste Trays

A drawing from a NASA report reveals the small chamber that Enos lived and worked in for 14 days. *NASA*

Was Enos training for a trip to the Moon? NASA refused to answer that question, but the timing made sense. It would take six days to travel to and from the Moon, plus another week for experiments. And while Enos did his two-week isolation test, NASA was negotiating a contract with North American Aviation to build a Moon ship.

Too Cool for Space School?

Unlike most astrochimps, Enos did not play well with people. NASA's report called him "one of the most excitable animals in his age group." Trainer Loren Bartrand described Enos as "standoffish and a rugged individualist." The chimp was also "moody and a little indifferent at times."

Unlike the younger astrochimps, Enos had no desire to play or snuggle with humans. Sergeant Dittmer tried to put a good spin on the astrochimp's reputation: "Enos was a good chimp, and he was smart, but he didn't take to people. . . . He wasn't really mean. He just didn't take to cuddling."

Enos was not a people pleaser either. "Just getting Enos into his space suit was a big challenge," says Vernon Pegram. "And sometimes it took four trainers to get him into his training chair. You'd think Enos would wash out of the program, but once he got settled, we had no problem at all. It turned out he was smart as a whip. He just wasn't excited to be doing the task."

For Enos, space school was not the free-flowing social group that wild chimps enjoyed. He could not leave and start his own troop if he disliked someone, or align himself with a dominant chimp to increase his power. The humans were the bosses here. Heck, they wouldn't even let him walk on his knuckles like a real chimp. The best Enos could do was resist his handlers and bite Ed Dittmer's fingers so hard that the sergeant thought he would lose them for a few painful seconds.

The astrochimp enjoyed a few more wild behaviors his trainers didn't like. Sometimes he dropped his diapers and exposed himself to people, and he threw poop at visitors.

Pad Leader Guenter Wendt gave tours of the Cape to VIPs on fact-finding missions. One day, a politician demanded to "see the monkeys."

"I told them they weren't monkeys, they were highly intelligent chimpanzees. But he insisted on seeing the monkeys," Wendt recalled. Enos was the only chimp there, and he had just returned from a long training session. "When those chimps didn't do what they were supposed to do, they'd receive a little shock through their feet," Wendt said. "So I knew this wasn't a good time to see Enos. But this guy said, 'I'm a congressman, and I want to see the monkeys.' So I took him, even though I knew exactly what was going to happen."

Enos glared at the politician, his upper lip bulging in red-hot rage.

"So that's the astronaut, eh?"

Growls rumbled through the room. How dare this stranger trespass in his territory! Enos shook the bars on his cage.

"What are you doing in there, little spaceman?" the congressman mocked.

Enos had had enough. He backed up, squatted, and pooped into his hand. Then he threw his handful of fresh feces at the congressman. *Splat!* The white dress shirt made a great target, even from 15 feet away.

Warm poop oozed down the congressman's shirt. Stunned, he leaned backward, trying to escape the smell. "Oh. I guess I know now why you didn't want me to go in."

The astrochimp's pranks were more proof of his high IQ. Chimps who throw feces (and hit their targets) are smarter, with larger left brains. They're also better at sharing information with other chimps. Take that, Mr. Congressman.

Another Chimp Countdown!

Enos's flight day, November 29, 1961, started like Ham's. He ate a small breakfast at 3:30 AM. Trainers dressed him in diapers and his space suit. Then they trimmed his whiskers so he would look cuter in press photos.

After a physical exam, the five-year-old astrochimp received flight clearance, and a medical van drove him to the launchpad. A veterinarian hooked Enos to medical sensors to measure his temperature and breathing. Next, vets placed a balloon catheter into Enos's bladder to collect urine. They inflated the balloon to hold it in place.

Now it was time for some new medical technology. To take blood pressure readings in space, veterinarians needed details from *inside* Enos's blood vessels. First, they angled a needle into a lower leg artery and inserted a thin wire through the needle. They eased a small plastic tube over the wire and attached the wire to a sensor taped onto Enos's skin. Then they repeated the steps with a leg vein.

Technicians placed the astrochimp in his couch, clicking seatbelts across his waist and chest. Then they crisscrossed his leg laces. They bolted the lid to his couch shut and turned on the environmental control system.

NASA chose Rocky as the backup astrochimp for Enos's flight. Rocky was named after a famous professional boxer because he boxed with his trainers. He also had cauliflower-shaped ears, as many boxers and wrestlers do. *NASA*

Finally, technicians carried Enos to the gantry, where the elevator lifted him up to the Mercury spacecraft.

Veterinarians then turned their attention to Rocky, who would replace Enos at the last minute if needed. No one trimmed the younger chimp's whiskers.

At 4:14 AM, Enos sat alone in the spacecraft. His waiting game began.

From the ground below, veterinarians watched the astrochimp's vital signs. So far, so good.

The Mercury Seven astronauts talked to each other—but not to Enos—as the clock ticked down. Alan Shepard worked CapCom in Bermuda, while Gordon Cooper did CapCom duty in California.

At Australia's western tracking station, Wally Schirra served as CapCom. When he'd arrived at the station a few hours earlier, he found a banana "quietly and thoughtfully" sitting in the middle of each desk. The bananas were both a joke and a gesture of respect to Enos, the astronaut they would track. Enos might have preferred an astrochimp CapCom.

At 7:40 AM, the countdown stopped when Mission Control lost contact with the spacecraft. Technicians unbolted the spacecraft's hatch to investigate. Enos's blood pressure spiked. He would have thrown poop at them if he could!

Once technicians found the problem—an on-off switch in the wrong position—the repair was simple. In Mission Control, someone joked that Enos must have flipped the switch off because Ham told him not to go.

Ninety minutes later, technicians re-bolted the space-craft's hatch and moved the gantry away. The count-down resumed.

Enos blasts into space on top of the powerful Atlas rocket. Note the escape tower above the spacecraft. The tower had its own small rocket, which could propel a human astronaut and the spacecraft away from the Atlas in last-minute emergencies. *NASA*

Stress soaked the air. The week before, an Atlas rocket carrying a squirrel monkey named Goliath exploded soon after liftoff. And a few weeks earlier, a small satellite designed to test the tracking system went off course about 40 seconds into the flight, and the safety officer hit the red button to blow it up. Was the United States counting down to victory? Or to another fiery failure?

At 10:06 AM, Enos started lever tests. He answered the same questions he'd done during his 14-day isolation experiment.

Two minutes later, the Atlas rocket fired Enos off the launchpad. About 100 miles up, the rocket curved into orbit, as 7.6 g slammed the astrochimp against his couch.

A few minutes later, the booster rocket fell away, and Enos began his first trip around Earth. The flight plan called for three orbits, each one taking about 100 minutes.

Tracking stations around the world watched Enos move across their maps. A red triangle pointed to where he would splash down if his retro-rockets fired at that moment.

As Enos recovered from the g-force, his pulse and blood pressure went down. He was more relaxed during this part of his trip than in two recent training sessions. Maybe his astrochimp skills were paying off?

The astrochimp earned 13 banana pellets by counting to 50. The star student also scored 47 water drinks, making only two mistakes.

While Enos orbited Earth, President Kennedy held a press conference. Mission Control called the president's press secretary with an update. The press secretary, in turn, passed President Kennedy a note. Curious reporters leaned forward as the president read a message from Enos: The chimpanzee "reports that everything is perfect and working well." Everyone laughed.

Twelve Seconds to Spare

Soon, everything changed.

During Enos's second orbit, electrical problems blocked his middle test lever from registering answers.

A glimpse into a Mercury Mission Control room. As Enos traveled around Earth, tracking stations would pick up his signal when he passed into their range. *NASA*

Enos received more than 75 shocks for *correct* answers. Like any good scientist, Enos experimented with levers and buttons, searching for a loophole in the circuits.

The electrical problem started to affect the air system, heating the cabin. The astrochimp's body temperature began rising. If Enos were talking to President Kennedy now, no one would be laughing.

As Enos flew on, an Australian tracking station reported problems with the electrical system and the gas jets. The spacecraft kept drifting higher and then lower. If the spacecraft did not face the right way (34 degrees above the horizon) when the retro-rockets fired, Enos could end up on Mars . . . or in another galaxy. The automatic system moved the spacecraft back into position each time it veered offtrack, burning extra fuel.

Details flew in from all directions. Could Enos survive a third trip around Earth?

Veterinarians and doctors weighed in. The astrochimp's temperature had climbed from 96 to 102 degrees Fahrenheit. His heart monitor showed some weird misbeats, but this was normal for Enos. His blood pressure measured high too, but not too high. For now, Enos could safely stay in space. Just barely.

Engineer and flight director Chris Kraft alerted the tracking stations: "All sites, this is Cape Flight. Repeat, Cape Flight. We have several situations for immediate— repeat, immediate—attention." He told them watch for electrical, temperature, and chimp problems.

"All sites, monitor and report immediately," said Flight Director Kraft. Urgency quivered in his voice. "Repeat, report immediately."

Enos kept flying.

The stations' updates brought good news and bad. The cabin temperature had stopped rising, but the gas jets kept acting up. If the jets kept moving Enos off track, the astrochimp's spacecraft wouldn't have enough fuel to return to Earth.

To bring Enos down early, one of the two remaining tracking stations would need to send a radar signal from the ground to fire the spacecraft's retro-rockets. The timing was tricky: stations could only send radar signals when the spacecraft flew in their radar range.

Director Chris Kraft called the stations in Hawai'i and California, and asked them to stay on the line.

Now was the time to talk to Hawai'i. But Director Kraft didn't give the order to fire the retro-rockets. He needed more time to think.

Ticktock.

Enos blazed past Hawai'i at 17,500 miles per hour.

Ticktock.

Enos flew toward the California station. This was it: the last chance to save the astrochimp from a third orbit.

Did the spacecraft have enough fuel? The question made frantic loops through the director's mind, around and around. If the fuel ran out, they couldn't control the spacecraft's landing site or speed. In other words, the astrochimp would crash.

Director Kraft couldn't risk it. With 12 seconds to spare, he gave orders to the California station: "Retro-fire on my mark . . . four, three, two, one, *mark!*" If the order had come any later, the spacecraft would have traveled too far to receive a radar signal, sending Enos around Earth again.

In his book *Flight: My Life in Mission Control*, Director Kraft described the atmosphere in Mission Control during the astrochimp's second orbit. "In those last minutes, all that mattered was getting [Enos] home safely. I don't remember thinking of him as a chimp. He was my responsibility as much as any [human] astronaut would ever be."

Fighting Mad

Enos fell out of orbit. His pounding heart drove his blood pressure higher.

On the ground, Mission Control workers stared at their radar screens.

A search plane circled the landing zone target, about 200 miles south of Bermuda. Seventeen navy recovery ships and search planes waited in the Atlantic Ocean.

Finally! The plane's pilot and copilot saw an orange, striped parachute, about 5,000 feet above the ocean surface. The plane radioed the splashdown site to nearby search ships. Good news! The spacecraft was floating!

After splashdown, the astrochimp did lever tests for 10 minutes. Then, his test screen went blank.

Enos waited. And waited.

Perhaps he was angry over the foot shocks, or stressed from the heat, but Enos was done waiting. He broke into the cover panel across his stomach. And tore down the special space suit zipper that NASA designed to resist 400 pounds of pressure. Then Enos ripped off the bio-sensors on his chest and legs. *Take that, Mission Control. Who's in charge now?*

Enos moved next to his urinary catheter, pulling it out. Remember the catheter's balloon, which veterinarians inflated to keep the tube from slipping out of his bladder? *Ye-ouch!*

About 75 minutes later, a helicopter picked up the astrochimp and flew him over the sea.

Finally, the copter lowered Enos onto the deck of the USS *Stormes*. Sailors and NASA officials gathered around the spacecraft. Their first priority? Blow open the hatch and unbolt the couch window to give Enos cool air and oxygen.

For three more hours, Enos lay in the couch as technicians struggled to free him.

The official NASA report said Enos was "fatigued but alert" when he left his couch. G. Merritt Preston, a NASA engineer, described Enos another way: "When he got back to the ground, he was just so mad he could—I mean, he was fighting mad."

Enos wobbled, unsteady on his feet, his face flushing in heat. Then he jumped up and down. Was he celebrating? Or trying to cool off?

When Enos saw Sergeant Dittmer, he ran through the crowds and leaped into the sergeant's arms! People who knew the astrochimp stared at each other, shocked. This wasn't the Enos they knew, but maybe he needed consoling?

Treats and Puzzles

Curious, Airman Willie Ogden tasted a banana pellet from the bag . . . *Hmmm, very fruity.* Then he handed a pellet treat to the chimp beside him.

The airman started to work. He removed the astrochimp's boots first. Enos crinkled his toes and jabbered. Then Ogden fumbled with the space suit. It hung loosely against the chimp's hair, soaked in sweat. A sailor rushed in with a telegram. "What's your opinion?" the note asked. "How's the research subject?"

Willie Ogden knew nothing about chimpanzees. He inspected chickens and cows for his regular air force job. Years before, he had worked with sentry dogs. But when a vet tech injured his back at the last minute, Ogden's boss sent him home to pack a suitcase. Don't tell anyone, his boss told him, but you're flying to Virginia to connect with the USS *Stormes.*

Now, less than 24 hours later, Ogden stared at America's first orbital astronaut. Enos stared back. The astrochimp looked parched. He must be thirsty. A fresh orange always hit the spot for Ogden on a hot day. Enos might like one, too. "Go to the kitchen and get some fruit," he told a sailor.

The airman cut the fruit in quarters and slipped an orange slice under Enos's lower lip. *Ahhhhh.*

Willie Ogden turned back to work. His most important job? Measure the wires the veterinarian removed from Enos's blood vessels. NASA doctors needed to make sure every bit of wire that went into the chimp early this morning came back out. The measurements had to match—exactly. Yes, yes, the numbers were right. "Measure again," said the vet. And again.

As the vet stitched closed the small openings in the astrochimp's legs, Ogden calmed Enos with head scratches and back rubs. And he kept the fruit coming: orange, apple, orange, apple, orange, apple. Distracted, Enos ignored the humans, savoring each fruit's juice, skin, and pulp.

Ogden and the veterinarian moved through a checklist as sailors rushed in with more telegrams. *Do this! Do that!* Ogden stuffed the papers in his pockets, choosing to soothe Enos instead.

After they finished, Ogden and the vet moved Enos to a steel cage. The vet left to start his reports, and Ogden sat down near Enos to fill out forms. The airman pulled out the telegrams and read through them. *Yes, we did that one. Yup, we did that, too. Whoops, we haven't done that yet.*

The airman glanced down to think. He should start a to-do list. Then a movement caught his eye. Enos held

two fingers through the cage, offering Ogden a present.
The airman accepted the gift, then studied Enos. Where'd
he get a piece of thread? *Oh, no. No, he couldn't have—*

Oh, yes, he did. Enos had untied his surgical knots
and removed the stitches. A moment later, Enos handed
Ogden another gift: the thread from his other leg.

Maybe he's bored, Ogden remembers thinking. "If you
like untying knots so much," he told Enos, "I'll find you
something better." Ogden sent a sailor for some rope and
then tied knots down the 10-foot length. He lowered the
rope into the cage and returned to his forms.

Twenty minutes later, Enos pushed the rope back
through the cage, every knot untied. Back and forth, the
rope game continued. Ogden knotted the rope and gave
it to Enos; Enos untied the knots and gave the rope back
to Ogden.

Later in the day, Enos flew to an air force hospital in
Bermuda for a longer exam. Bigwigs from the air force
and NASA crowded onto the second floor, watching the
astrochimp. Chief Veterinarian Jerry Fineg listened to
Enos's lungs and heart and tested his reflexes. Had three
hours in microgravity injured Enos?

A reporter came by for news. Was the astrochimp
OK?

Yes!

Photos! The world wanted photos! Dr. Fineg gripped
Enos by the arm, bracing himself against the exam table
and a nearby wall. A second vet held the chimp's other
arm. Dr. Fineg tried to smile, but he couldn't smile and

concentrate at the same time. Keeping Enos in check was a four-person job on a good day, but four adults holding down America's first orbital astronaut would look bad. Dr. Fineg held tighter. If Enos decided to leap or bite, he knew they couldn't stop him.

After the picture session, Dr. Fineg and the VIPs left to study the reports. Two veterinarians stayed behind with Enos, watching for signs that space had changed the chimp. Veterinarians and doctors poured over Enos's high blood pressure and erratic heart data. Thankfully, electrical problems caused the scary numbers, not space travel.

The astrochimp flight answered NASA's questions: high altitudes were safe for humans, and doctors could stop worrying about boiling blood and popping eyes.

Enos did so well on his lever tests that NASA believed humans could concentrate in deep space. Their reflexes would stay sharp and their muscles strong. Enos's trip also showed engineers that the spacecrafts were strong enough to protect astronauts from heat and radiation.

Shortly after Enos's flight, NASA announced another orbital trip, this time with a human astronaut on board. Pack your bags, Colonel Glenn!

No Flame, No Glory

Americans may have celebrated their move forward in the Space Race, but they did not adore Enos the way they did Ham. Ham's postflight photos showed him riding on a trainer's hip, all snuggled in like a happy toddler, basking in the attention. Enos, in contrast, was Joe Cool. He didn't care that he'd just made two trips around Earth. He wouldn't pose pretty for photos, and he certainly wouldn't let humans carry him around like a baby.

When NASA flew Enos back to Cape Canaveral for an airport press conference, Sergeant Dittmer and another officer guided the astrochimp off the plane on

Sergeant Dittmer and an assistant pose for photographers with Enos. After a few minutes, Enos became bored and sat down. *NASA, National Archives*

wrist straps. As they walked down the stairs, the officers stopped for pictures. Click—*flassssshhhhhh*—click,
the cameras threatened. Enos tensed, warning photographers with his best predator stare.

Sergeant Dittmer tightened his grip on the chimp's
wrist. Slowly, the sergeant reached his other hand over
to scratch Enos's chin. Would a good scratch distract the
chimp? Nope. A trip to outer space had not changed one
thing for Enos: a human hand was an invitation to bite!
The sergeant moved his fingers just in time.

After a few minutes, Enos relaxed, but he didn't ham
it up for reporters. Instead, the astrochimp sat down on
the lowest step and waited. Why waste energy standing? News stories said, "Enos showed himself to be a cut
above the circus performing chimp by refusing to mug
for the camera, do cartwheels or otherwise debase his
position as the first two-legged American to orbit earth."
Instead, Enos "fended off the press with a polite calm,"
LIFE magazine said.

Later in the day, Airman Ogden stopped by to visit
Enos before NASA sent the astrochimps back to New
Mexico. "I knew I'd never see him again and wanted
to say goodbye." They went outside and sat in the
sunshine. The airman rubbed the chimp's head and
dropped banana pellets at his feet. Every few minutes,
Enos scooted closer. Where was the chimp who didn't
like people? The pair seemed more like Sergeant Dittmer and Ham. "I didn't train Enos, that's for sure," Willie Ogden recalls. "He trained me."

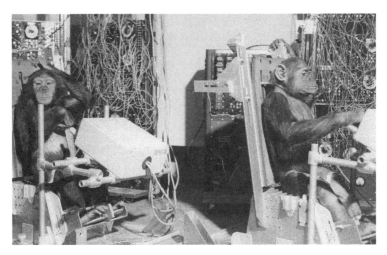

Astrochimps Ham (left) and Enos answer color, counting, and shape questions after Enos's orbital flight. NASA wanted to find out whether time in space affected their test scores. Nearby computers (note their size and number of wires!) generated the preprogrammed questions. *US Air Force, New Mexico Museum of Space History*

Human Versus Chimp?

Enos flew faster, higher, and farther than Ham, but he wasn't a star. He also traveled *around* Earth in deep space—not in a low-space arc. And his lever tests were much harder than Ham's tests. Still, Enos was not as popular as Ham. Not even close. *Life* magazine gave him a caption instead of a front cover.

Science writer Mary Roach did the math while researching her space book *Packing for Mars*. Ham received about five times more news coverage than Enos. Maybe Americans liked their astrochimps cute and playful, like Ham? Or had the country had shifted its focus to human astronauts?

In the weeks before his trip, Colonel Glenn did many interviews. America wanted to know *more! more! more!* about the astronaut who would help the United States catch the Soviets. Just a few years earlier, John Glenn set a national speed record flying from California to New York, landing him in parades, newspapers, and even a TV game show. He knew the secret to fame: smile for the cameras and tell good stories.

The colonel ignored the astrochimps when he talked with reporters. He didn't mention the electrical problems on Enos's trip either. Instead, Colonel Glenn bragged about the Mercury Seven. "I have talked to people who seem to think that an astronaut must be either very afraid or slightly crazy. Actually, there's nothing spooky or supernatural about space flight. Like any flying, it is simply a product of human skill."

Despite their public comments, the Mercury Seven astronauts knew the truth. They were still competing with those comical apes. Even fellow pilots teased Colonel Glenn about "following a chimp." And the human versus chimp Space Race could get worse. NASA's new Mark II Moon plan called for two-week trips with two astronauts on board: a human *and* an astrochimp!

Ready to Fly

Astronauts live with delays. They come with the job. Enos's flight date changed once, to fix a hydrogen peroxide leak. NASA changed Colonel Glenn's flight day *10* times.

Hungry for space stories, more than 600 reporters waited at the Cape instead of going home after each cancellation. The nearest town, Cocoa Beach, did not have enough hotel rooms, so most reporters slept in their cars. Only the mosquitoes were happy.

To relax, people made chimp jokes. They couldn't help themselves. A cartoon showed Ham and Enos leaving a Mercury spacecraft with the caption "We're a little behind the Russians and a little ahead of the Americans." In another, an astrochimp warned human astronauts that space would make them crave bananas.

One chimp trainer wrote a limerick and sent it to John Glenn:

> *I will say it again and again*
> *If you don't think I'm right, ask John Glenn*
> *That his wisest of tips*
> *Came from chimpanzee's lips*
> *From old Enos and Ham, not from men.*

Finally, on February 20, 1962, it looked like John Glenn would really fly. The colonel waited in his *Friendship 7* spacecraft for more than three hours.

The whole world waited, hovering near radios and TVs. To distract himself, Colonel Glenn did deep-breathing and muscle-tensing exercises in between spacecraft checks.

More than 1,000 television and newspaper reporters crowded onto Cape Canaveral. About 50,000 people—nicknamed "bird watchers"—gathered on south Florida beaches. Thousands more stood in their driveways, waiting for liftoff.

At 9:47 AM, an Atlas rocket blasted Colonel Glenn into space. Every 40 minutes, Colonel Glenn flew through sunlight to darkness and back again. His Mercury Seven friends kept him company. Alan Shepard worked Cap-Com in Florida, Wally Schirra in California, Gordon Cooper in Australia, and Gus Grissom in Bermuda.

After enduring more than 7 *g* of entry force, Colonel John Glenn orbits Earth in microgravity. *NASA*

When Colonel Glenn flew over Perth, a small city in western Australia, he got a fun surprise. Instead of a dark, sleeping city, people had left their lights on to say hello. Perth had a special relationship with NASA because the western Australia station may have saved the astrochimp's life when it noticed the spacecraft's electrical problems. Perth's lights also served as an experiment, proving that astronauts could see house lights from space. Soon after, Perth became known as the City of Light.

NASA filled John Glenn's flight with tests to measure his strength, vision, reflexes, and thinking skills in space. Twice an hour, Colonel Glenn did rowing exercises with a bungee cord, one row per second for 30 seconds.

Colonel Glenn used the fingertip lights in his gloves to move light spots north, south, east, and west, following the light with each eye. He read letters on an eye chart too. Just like the Astrochimps' lever tests, Colonel Glenn's vision tests were not busywork. If human astronauts couldn't see well in orbital space, NASA could still bring them home with remote control radio signals. Those signals would not be strong enough to reach the far side of the Moon, however, so NASA had to know how space affected sight.

Could he keep track of time in 0 g? Performing his tests on schedule would answer that question.

Enos proved that astronauts could eat and drink in space, but NASA had new questions now. Would 0 g affect how fast the body digests food? To find out, they gave Colonel Glenn chocolate malt and sugar pills to measure digestion speeds.

NASA also needed to learn how to feed astronauts on long Moon flights and whether deep space would make astronauts burn more calories. Colonel Glenn said the astronauts "joked about taking along some normal food such as a ham sandwich." Instead of a sandwich, Colonel Glenn got two large toothpaste tubes—one filled with applesauce and the other with beef stew. He ate his meal with straws.

And Around We Go!

Colonel Glenn's yaw thrusters kept failing during the first orbit, letting the spacecraft's nose drift off course. The automatic mode moved the spacecraft back on track each time, wasting precious fuel. Finally, Mission Control told Colonel Glenn to turn off the thrusters and fly in manual mode.

On the second orbit, the environmental control system acted up. The Kano and Zanzibar stations reported a sudden 12 percent drop in oxygen. Glenn said he felt "comfortably warm" inside his space suit. He cooled his suit with a hand control, something Enos couldn't do.

Near the end of Glenn's last orbit, a red warning light flashed on one of Mission Control's computer screens. The Segment 51 light said the heat shield had loosened. Mission Control asked Glenn if he'd heard any loud sounds. (A loose heat shield would have made noise when the steering thrusters fired.) No, he had not.

If an astrochimp were flying *Friendship 7*, Mission Control would have been helpless. But a human astronaut gave them more options. NASA told Colonel Glenn not to release the retro-rockets after he fired them. The rockets might hold the heat shield in place.

Mission Control workers watched their radar screens. From Enos's flight, they knew the spacecraft would go quiet as it flew through the blackout zone. But they had to wonder: Was Colonel Glenn still alive? If the heat shield fell off, his radar beeps would never return.

Radio and television stations announced the details like the final moments of the Super Bowl. People around the world had the same scary thought: Were flames tearing through Glenn's spacecraft as it sped through Earth's atmosphere?

Silence. Silence. More silence.

Suddenly, the radar screens lit up! "Boy, that was a real fireball of a ride," Glenn shouted. Parachutes softened his splashdown, and rescue helicopters swept in.

A few days later, President Kennedy invited the Mercury Seven astronauts and their families to a big party at the White House. The human astronauts expected cheers and compliments. Instead, the president's daughter reminded them that the astrochimps were first in space. When Caroline Kennedy saw Colonel Glenn, she asked, "Where's the monkey?"

BATTLE OF THE ASTRONAUTS

At every turn, competition fueled the Space Race. It wasn't just the United States versus the Soviet Union. It was US astronaut versus Soviet cosmonaut. Dog versus human versus chimpanzee. Male versus female.

The Mercury Seven astronauts fought private Space Races, too, competing for bragging rights and spaceflights. NASA's favorite astronauts, the Gold Team members, worked hard to stay there—they would go to space first. Their rivals on the Red Team battled to move up.

At first, the Mercury Seven didn't view the astrochimps as competition. Those stinky chimpanzees were just passengers. But to their dismay, Americans took the astrochimps seriously. People couldn't get enough of them. Pictures! Stories! Autographs! *Give us more!*

For some astronauts, competing with the astro-chimps was downright infuriating. The human astro-nauts could have offered the chimps respect, or at least pretended. They knew how Ham's 17 g of entry force felt. They also knew how nerve-racking it was to won-der whether the rescue team would find you before the spacecraft sank. Didn't the Mercury Seven astronauts value the ways the chimps made their trips safer? Were they that jealous of the chimps' fame? Or were they just too sensitive to cartoons and jokes?

NASA's engineers didn't like chimp jokes either. Wal-ter Schirra, who made America's third orbital trip, made a chimp joke in space. "I alienated some of the flight con-trollers because, after drifting for a while, I put it back into automatic control [and said], 'I'm in chimp mode now'; it didn't go over too well."

In the Numbers

After each flight, scientists spent thousands of hours comparing details from the Mercury Seven astronauts, the Soviet cosmonauts, and the astrochimps. The fol-lowing data shows how the astrochimps compare with the human astronauts.

G-Forces

Ham endured stronger entry and reentry g-forces than any Space Race astronaut, including Enos and the Rus-sian cosmonauts. The astrochimps did g-force training, but the humans knew tricks to fight the pain. They tensed the muscles in their legs and stomachs and grunted out the air trapped in their lungs.

Faster, Farther, Higher

In the suborbital flights, Ham flew faster, farther, higher, and longer than the human astronauts. In the

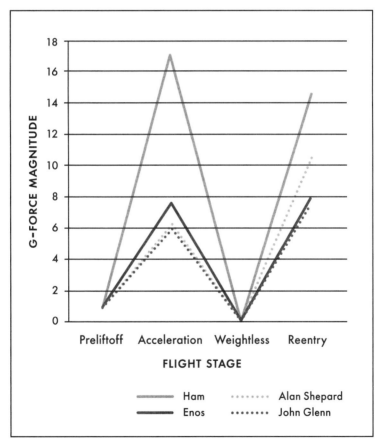

This graph shows the g-forces the early Mercury astronauts endured during each flight stage.

early orbital flights, Enos outflew John Glenn and Yuri Gagarin.

Zero G

In suborbital space, Ham spent the most time in zero gravity. In orbital space, Soviet cosmonaut Gherman Titov won this race. He spent most of his 25-plus-hour mission in 0 g. (It might seem like 0 g would be a relief from strong g-forces, but many astronauts get queasy or throw up in 0 g.)

Vital Victories

NASA's veterinarians and doctors also compared the astronauts, but as a learning tool, not to mock or gossip. Changes in an astronaut's vital signs and blood chemistry could help NASA understand how space affects animal hearts, brains, eyes, and more.

The Mercury Seven astronauts compared their vital signs for another reason. Every astronaut wanted to appear calm and brave. But if their heart rate or blood pressure changed a lot in space, people would know they were secretly fighting fear—or terror.

The Soviets used pulse and respiration rates to compare their cosmonauts too. In the first minute after launch, when facing only 4 g, cosmonaut Yuri Gagarin's pulse shot up from 64 beats a minute to 150 beats a minute. The Mercury Seven astronauts snickered at this change. Gagarin may have looked calm after his flight, but his racing heart rate said otherwise.

In some flight stages, the chimps and humans showed the same pulse changes. All pulse rates increased during

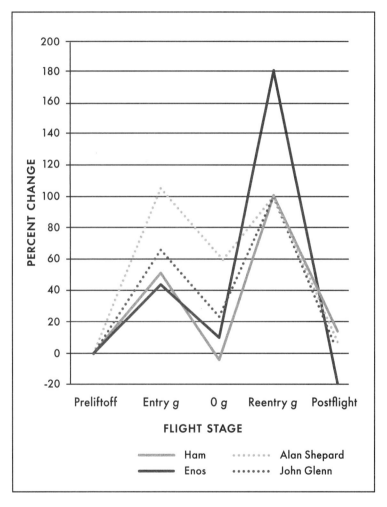

This graph shows how each astronaut's pulse rate changed during different flight stages. Enos's pulse rate changed the most.

entry g-forces. They all went down during 0 *g*, and back up during reentry g-forces. Ham, Alan Shepard, and John Glenn showed similar increases: 94, 96, and 97 percent, respectively. Enos's pulse rate changed the most. During reentry *g*, his heart raced 179 percent faster than usual!

Stressed in Space

Another way to measure stress is to study blood cells under a microscope. Like other animals, humans and chimpanzees quickly make more white blood cells (WBCs) when stressed.

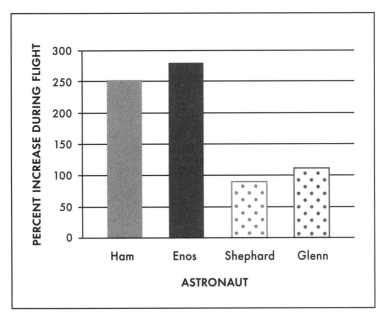

This graph shows how much each astronaut's white blood cell count increased during their spaceflight. White blood cells (WBCs) help measure stress in chimpanzees and humans.

Alan Shepard and John Glenn doubled their WBCs during their trips. Ham and Enos almost *quadrupled* their WBCs. Remember, both Ham and Alan Shepard flew much shorter trips than Enos and John Glenn (minutes compared to hours), so their bodies had less time to make these stress-fighting cells.

Why did human and chimpanzee astronauts have such different stress responses? No one knows for sure. Perhaps landing and recovery startled the chimps? They hadn't practiced these parts of their missions.

The human astronauts also talked with friends and coworkers during their flights. These chats may have helped their bodies relax. Alan Shepard and John Glenn knew the rescue helicopters would pick them up in a few minutes. The astrochimps waited alone for hours.

Coolest Cat

Early in his flight, Enos was one cool cat. Before liftoff, his biosensors reported below-normal blood pressure and breathing rates. During his first orbit, the astrochimp was more relaxed than during centrifuge training.

Enos's blood pressure and breathing rates jumped during his second orbit. They stayed high until he ripped off his biosensors after splashdown, ending NASA's data stream. A few hours after his rescue, Enos regained his cool-cat status with a pulse rate 20 percent *lower* than his usual resting rate. No other Mercury astronaut can make this claim!

Hot-Blooded

When Enos flew, both the cabin *and* his couch over-heated, causing his body temperature to go up more than 6 percent. A 6 percent increase may sound small, but brains are sensitive to heat. Even small changes can cause a lot of damage.

John Glenn's spacecraft overheated, too, but his body temperature went up just 1 percent. His space suit kept him cool.

As NASA would learn over the years, animal blood doesn't bubble or boil in pressurized spacecrafts, but 0 *g* does cause problems for astronauts. On Earth, gravity pushes blood down to the legs. The heart fights gravity, pumping blood upward.

In space, blood pools higher in the body, giving astronauts puffy faces. Astronauts also return from space with less blood and fewer red blood cells. They may feel dizzy from the extra blood pooled in their heads. When astronauts stay in space for a while, their hearts can weaken because their heart muscles don't work as hard. (Once astronauts return to Earth, their hearts get stronger again.) However, Ham, Enos, and the human Mercury astronauts did not stay in space long enough to have these problems.

ASTROCHIMPS ON THE MOON?

After John Glenn's orbital flight, Americans relaxed a little. Was the United States pulling ahead in the Space Race? Or at least catching up?

The Soviets answered these questions a few months later. Cosmonauts Pavel Popovich and Andrian Nikolayev orbited Earth at the *same time* in *different* spacecrafts for *days*. At one point, they were only a few miles apart!

News writers begged Americans to understand the urgency of the space gap. "If this were just a peaceful game with prestige as the only prize, perhaps it wouldn't matter who wins," one story argued. "But the military implications, fantastic as they seem, are of staggering importance. The nation that controls space can control the Earth. Big space ships armed with nuclear weapons could demolish a continent. . . . We must put more muscle behind our effort. We must gain the lead—soon—and hold it."

America may have lost the first rounds of the Space Race, but the battle wasn't over. If NASA moved the finish line to the Moon, the United States could still win. To compete, NASA revved up its new Gemini and Apollo space programs with stronger rockets and bigger spacecrafts.

Would the astrochimps beta test Moon flights? People wanted to know. NASA and Holloman Air Force Base said, "No comment," but their actions said yes. The US government gave Holloman $1 million to build Chimp College, a high-tech training center with large classrooms and labs.

By the summer of 1962, Chimp College was no longer a secret. A national headline teased: "Chimponaut May Be 1st to Plant Flag on the Moon." Cartoons showed astrochimps on the Moon, holding American flags. Even a new Disney movie, *Moon Pilot*, showcased a chimpanzee in space.

Outrage surged through the human astronauts—again. Those stinky chimpanzees might get the country's first Moon flights? *Un-be-lie-va-ble.*

Moon School

Ham, Minnie, and the other astrochimps kept training at Chimp College, charming visitors, making new friends, and learning new skills too. Chimp College was harder than Mercury space school. Chimps worked with five light colors now, and sounds. Computers made high-pitched squeals through a voice plate. Chimps hit the plate at just the right time to stop the noise.

Enos had other plans. A reporter who toured the college said Enos must have "read his press clippings," becoming even more headstrong. When a photographer tried to pose Ham and Enos together in their space couches, Enos bit his handler's bottom. "Only a wallet in the [handler's] rear pocket prevented serious injury," the writer said.

Another Chimp College student, six-year-old Bobby Joe, wowed the world. He could "pilot a spacecraft back through the Earth's atmosphere after a trip into space." Bobby Joe used two levers like a video game. One hand moved a cross up and down; the other hand moved the cross left and right. When Bobby Joe kept the cross inside a moving circle for two 10-second trials, he got a banana pellet. In a five-hour class, Bobby Joe easily earned 225 banana treats!

Many people did not believe chimpanzees could fly themselves to the Moon. Major Herbert Reynolds, chief of Holloman's psychology research, tried to convince them: "There is no question about it. [Bobby Joe] would guide a space vehicle into space and bring it back. He can sit and track for hours. His eyes do not tire too much. We hope he will get a chance."

The astrochimps weren't always serious students. They lived for the moments when something distracted a trainer. Fast as a flash, the chimps grabbed anything in reach with their hands or feet—car keys, eyeglasses, tools—and hid it. The chimps kept straight faces while trainers searched, snickering to themselves. Soon, the whole class erupted in chuckles and guffaws, and trainers knew they'd been pranked. Again.

Treat stashes were fair game too. If a trainer answered a phone call or took a bathroom break, chimps quickly rearranged boxes into step stools. They raced up the countertops and tore open the cabinets—*wahoo!*—fruit, candy, and gum galore!

One day, Bobby Joe used his locksmith skills to escape from his holding cage. Quietly, he crept down the hall to the room where the college stored the banana treats. "Bobby Joe knew what he wanted," said Master Sergeant Joe Murray. "He opened the door, grabbed a sack of pellets, and ran down the [row of] cages throwing handfuls of food to the chimps . . . They were all chattering, and the handlers were running after Bobby Joe, but he kept throwing the pellets to his buddies. Finally, when he reached the end of the cages, he sat down to eat some of his ill-gotten gains himself, but they were all gone. He had given them all away."

After dinner, the chimps sat around small tables for their new favorite treat: a fizzing bottle of cold soda. Trainers passed out the sodas one at a time, giving the first bottle to a different chimp each day. The chimps always knew whose turn it was to get the first bottle, the second bottle, and so on, waiting patiently for their drink.

The chimps' antics reminded Sergeant Dittmer of his five young children. What could he do but laugh? The other trainers laughed too. Working with the chimps became a "highly sought-after assignment," says veterinarian Bill Britz. "No one wanted to be reassigned. People often stayed on as civilians after their military service ended."

Training People

While trainers taught the astrochimps new skills, Ham trained some new humans.

In May 1963, two months after NASA closed the Mercury space program, the air force dismissed Ham from Chimp College. Instead of flying to the Moon, Ham went to the National Zoo in Washington, DC.

Quickly, the astrochimp became the zoo's star attraction. Visitors came by the thousands. So did letters asking for Ham's handprints. The zoo painted Ham's new home in air force blue and built bleachers for visitors in the grassy area near his cage.

Ham dazzled fans with leaps and spins, using parallel bars to swing round and round and upside down. He finished each show with a flourish, landing on a high shelf, glancing down at the starstruck crowds.

Ham's new humans didn't use classrooms or give tests. Melanie Bond, a primate keeper at the National Zoo, did special training with the great apes called reinforcement. This type of training works by rewarding good behaviors instead of punishing bad ones.

Bond taught a young orangutan named Junior to clean his cage by letting him play with her whistle as reinforcement and used food rewards to teach an older orangutan to play Simon Says. Once the orangutan learned the game, she played it with schoolchildren.

Bond also used reinforcement with Ham. One day after breakfast, she started to let Ham outside. When Ham realized he was going out, he handed Bond a celery stalk as a reward. Ham understood her training trick and reinforced it!

New Classes

Back at Chimp College, disappointment echoed through the halls. James Webb, NASA's director, said a chimp and human would share the two-seated Gemini spacecraft. *Wait a minute. . . they would share?* The human astronaut would pilot, while the astrochimp would collect health data, said NASA. *Didn't NASA know how smart Bobby Joe and Duane were?*

The astrochimps might not be pilots, but they did do complex work. Instead of counting to 50, like the early astrochimps, the chimps learned number symbols. George excelled at the new math tests. When a computer displayed a number from one through eight, George pressed his lever that many times. Chimps got a banana pellet treat for seven right answers in a row.

Trainers also added new shapes to the pattern tests. To learn dashes and Xs, chimps played tic-tac-toe. During marathon game sessions, losers glared at winners. Big

Mean, a female named for her "foul temper," once played 214 games in a row with Louie, winning 142 times! When Big Mean lost too many games in a row, she stamped her feet and sulked, refusing to play anymore.

Big Mean playing tic-tac-toe on a light panel. *US Air Force*

Big Mean met her match with Pale Face, though. Pale Face had flunked out of the Mercury space school. He couldn't sit still long enough to learn the levers. Trainers described him as "too excited and unruly." But Pale Face loved tic-tac-toe. He even beat an air force general. Pale Face soon discovered the secret to playing with Big Mean and other sore losers: let them win once in a while. When trainers studied the game recordings, they found a pattern: Big Mean had to win about 20 percent of the games, or she quit. How did Pale Face figure that out?

As the chimps trained, psychologists discovered they still had a lot to learn about chimpanzees. Yes, the astrochimps liked banana treat rewards, but they enjoyed competing with one another and learning new skills even more. The chimps also liked showing off, making higher scores when people watched. Psychologists told trainers to stop using seat belts and foot shocks—there wasn't any point.

From the outside, Chimp College may have looked like fun and games. But inside, scientists used game results for compare-and-contrast experiments. NASA needed to know whether human astronauts could stay alert on Moon trips. Enos and a few human astronauts did well orbiting Earth, but eight days of microgravity, in much deeper space, might be dangerous—or deadly.

To find out, scientists sent the astrochimps on make-believe trips to outer space. Since Apollo spacecrafts would hold three astronauts, some chimps trained in pairs. They stayed in the lab for 24 hours. And the chimps tested in decompression chambers that mimicked the vacuum pressures of deep space. Trainers also added entry and reentry g-forces, just like real space trips.

Chimps did lever tests during the fake trips so scientists could compare their skills and speeds. On one fake flight, Bobby Joe pulled the correct lever 6,980 out of 7,000 times for a score of 99.7 percent. A visiting congressman did the same test and failed.

Chimp Glenda made five-day practice trips alone. The trips started with a high-speed zoom down the sled track, mimicking liftoff force. Then trainers moved Glenda to a decompression room, where she did lever tests and rested, as if she were orbiting Earth. During the first three days, Glenda made only two mistakes. After five days, scientists changed the air pressure to mimic a returning spacecraft and raced her back down the sled track to mimic reentry g-forces.

In June 1963 cosmonaut Valentina Tereshkova became the first woman in space, traveling 48 times around Earth. In this Space Race, the United States lagged far behind the Soviets. (Two decades later, the United States flew its first female astronaut, Dr. Sally Ride, on the space shuttle *Challenger* in 1983. It took another 12 years before an American female, Colonel Eileen Collins, piloted a spacecraft.)

If NASA had accepted pilot Jerrie Cobb's offer to trade places with an astrochimp, Cobb could have been the first American to orbit Earth *and* the first woman in space. Soon after cosmonaut Tereshkova's flight, newspaper writers asked the Mercury Seven astronauts about American women in space. The men laughed. "We could have flown her instead of the chimpanzee," said astronaut Gordon Cooper.

Changing Times

Soon, new animals joined the Space Race. NASA built tiny Moon buggies to beta test their new lunar vehicles. The drivers? Astro-mice, not chimps. France sent a cat on a 13-minute suborbital space trip. Félicette flew weightless for five minutes, and parachuted from the spacecraft before it crashed, as Soviet cosmonauts did.

Chimp College saw changes too. Sergeant Dittmer left the chimps to serve as a rescue medic teacher in Vietnam. Other Holloman staff also went to Vietnam. Dr. Britz and Dr. Pegram went back to school, and Dr. Fineg moved to a university to teach.

By now, more than 100 chimps lived at Holloman: a mix of adults, teenagers, toddlers, and infants. Older chimps brought new challenges to Holloman. "Adult chimps can be seven times stronger than humans," reminds Dr. Pegram. Trainers had to be very careful with the larger chimps: "It's four hands, not two, when they grab you."

The younger chimps also brought new problems. Little K, the first baby born at Chimp College, did well at first. His mom, Lady, took good care of him until trainers started bringing him solid foods. Lady removed the fruits and cereals every time. Maybe she did not trust people? Baby Josephine was born too early, and Phyllis's mom ignored her. (In the wild, females learn how to parent by watching other moms.) Babies who needed full-time care moved in with human families.

The air force designed new living spaces for the chimps. Their rooms now had toys, swinging perches, heat, light, and running water, and each room opened to an outdoor patio so chimps could spend more time with friends. Indoors, the air force built two circular living rooms with revolving doors at each end, making it easier for chimps to come and go as they liked and avoid troublemakers.

Outdoors, workers built a 30-acre playground with trees and shaded napping spots. Vernon Pegram and other trainers also dug an 18-foot-wide moat around the playground to serve as a natural fence. "Chimps can wade but they cannot swim," explains Dr. Pegram. "They sink like a stone in water because their muscles are so dense."

Around the moat, trainers added an electric fence to keep strange people and other animals away from the chimps. The moat worked when filled with water. But when water levels went down, trainers found chimps sitting on the electric fence, surveying the desert. Sometimes they climbed right over the fence.

The new living spaces would let the chimps live more like wild chimps, psychologists hoped. When the chimps weren't in class, they could choose their own friends and hang out where they liked. And since each area had more than one door, chimps could even avoid troublemakers. The plan fell apart at dinnertime; vicious fights broke out as larger males claimed the food as their territory.

Space Strolls

Like a fast-paced Ping-Pong game, the Space Race moved forward. Both countries sent more and more missions to space, testing new skills and technologies.

The next goal? Walking in space. An astrochimp in the copilot's seat gave NASA two options. The astrochimp could float in space while the human astronaut remained safely inside the spacecraft. Or the chimp could stay inside while the human astronaut ventured into space.

Neither option was perfect. "The problem in blasting a chimp into space and getting him outside the capsule [for a space walk]," said one scientist, "is how to make the chimp understand when to come back in. He might just decide he liked it out there."

Safety was another big issue. Bobby Joe and Duane could pilot the spacecraft, but how could they help in an emergency? A human copilot could talk to a space-walker and Mission Control, or pull the spacewalker back inside. It turned out, the human astronauts were safer without the astrochimps.

In March 1965 the Soviets crossed a new Space Race finish line: a cosmonaut walked in space for 12 minutes!

Ten weeks later, an American astronaut walked in space for eight minutes longer than the cosmonaut.

America forged forward. They could still win the big prize: landing on the Moon before the Soviets—*if* they worked harder *and* faster.

The next year, the Soviets scored another first: orbiting the Moon. The *Luna 10* spacecraft measured X-rays and gasses without a cosmonaut on board. The United States followed two months later, but its spacecraft, *American Surveyor 1,* landed *on* the Moon. The *Surveyor* also traveled without an astronaut and took more than 11,000 pictures.

In early 1967 a launchpad fire killed three American astronauts, including Gus Grissom. Grief weighed heavy through the country.

As astronaut safety became even more important to Americans, a wary NASA turned to the astrochimps again. Trainers measured and remeasured the chimps: arms, hands, legs, feet, waists, heads, necks. *Stand still, please!* NASA sent the numbers to the same company that made the human astronauts' Moon space suits.

Now the astrochimps started their days with a new routine: suiting up. Trainers moved in slow motion so the fabric wouldn't rip. First, the body suit went on, then the boots and gloves, and finally the helmet. The chimps wore the suits on Moon-trip experiments, training in strong g-forces, high pressures, and extreme temperatures.

The astrochimp Moon suits let NASA ask new research questions. Does breathing oxygen from inside the suit change how fast an astronaut can think and move? If a space suit rips, how long until the astronaut passes out? Why do astronauts get so tired "walking" in 0 gravity? The answers made space safer for America's human astronauts.

And the Winner Is . . .

A few months after America's launchpad fire, the Soviets sent a cosmonaut to space in *Soyuz 1*. The next day, three more cosmonauts launched in *Soyuz 2*. The Soviets had designed a complex space ballet. *Soyuz 2* would catch up with *Soyuz 1* as it orbited the Moon, then two of

Astrochimp during a space helmet fitting. *US Air Force, New Mexico Museum of Space History*

its cosmonauts would float over to *Soyuz 1*. If the Soviets pulled it off, they would move closer to getting the first humans on the Moon.

But the two Soviet spacecrafts did not connect. Instead, *Soyuz 1* lost power, sending the spacecraft home early. Then the main parachute failed, killing the cosmonaut in a high-speed crash. The Soviets tried to regroup, but more disasters followed. They watched a booster rocket explode on the launchpad and had to detonate a spacecraft that went off course.

America, in contrast, felt safer. Its Saturn rocket was strong and reliable. Astronauts had improved their skills, while engineers had honed the technology.

And then? *Not again!* In September 1968, the Soviets rebounded with another first: a spacecraft with two tortoises on board circled the Moon. The reptiles returned to Earth alive in a splash landing. Their spacecraft couldn't carry cosmonauts, but if the Soviets had a larger spacecraft ready to go, the Space Race would have ended soon thereafter.

Three weeks later, America launched human astronauts on *Apollo 7*. Their mission? Beta test the new Moon-travel systems while orbiting Earth. The astrochimps stayed home.

NASA's next mission, *Apollo 8*, called for more tests orbiting Earth. But the finish line glowed ahead—close, oh so close. Should America waste time on more tests? No one could forget the cautious mindset that had let the Soviets send a human to space first.

Soon, NASA changed its mind. Instead of making more trips around Earth, *Apollo 8*'s human astronauts would orbit the *Moon*!

In late December 1968, the Saturn V booster rocket blasted *Apollo 8* into space. The Saturn V was more than four times taller and almost 100 times more powerful than the Redstone rocket that sent Ham to space. *Apollo 8*'s astronauts became the first humans to see the far side of the Moon, and the world listened to the astronauts talk in two live broadcasts from lunar orbit.

Now trailing the United States, the Soviets scheduled a new mission to surge forward: another Moon trip to test a new booster rocket with a spacecraft large enough to carry humans. On July 3, 1969, near midnight, the Soviet's powerful new rocket lifted their hopes for victory into the dark sky.

Seconds later, the engines stopped. The rocket paused, hovering over the ground below. And then—*kaboom!*—the rocket and spacecraft exploded. Flames torched the launchpad. Windows shattered for miles. The Soviets stayed quiet, but they knew the harsh truth: this rocket problem could take years to fix.

Two weeks later, *Apollo 11* astronauts Neil Armstrong and Buzz Aldrin walked on the Moon. The Space Race that began with a Soviet satellite that terrified America ended when an American Moon lander broadcast the country's victory to the world, live from deep space.

FINAL FLIGHTS

When the Space Race ended, the human astronauts still had jobs. Alan Shepard hit a golf ball on the Moon. John Glenn became a US senator from Ohio and later ran for president.

The astrochimps lived different lives. Chimp College closed after America landed on the Moon, and the air force used the chimps to test seat belts and medicines. By now, more than 200 chimps lived in the New Mexico colony. Some were original astrochimps; others were astrochimp children and grandchildren.

In 1970 Congress told the air force to stop working with chimps. The government would no longer pay for research not related to the military. Congress gave

Holloman $500,000 in emergency money to support the chimps, but the funding ended there. Since the air force couldn't use the chimps anymore, they loaned them to research companies.

As the years passed, debates about the chimps heated up. Scientists, politicians, and animal rights groups protested together after a news show brought the chimps' story into people's living rooms. One of the research companies, the Coulston Foundation, had been cited many times for the bad ways they treated more than 600 chimps. The foundation received hate mail and death threats after the story aired.

In 1998 the air force labeled the chimps as "surplus government equipment." The chimps needed homes. But where could they go? The chimps couldn't return to African forests. They wouldn't know how to find food or avoid predators. Zoos didn't have room for them. And chimps don't make good pets.

Two groups tried to rescue the air force chimps. Primarily Primates bought 31 chimps. When the first 10 chimps arrived in southern Texas, workers enticed them from the truck with apples and marshmallows. The sanctuary's male chimps "strutted and posed" for the newcomers.

Dr. Carole Noon, a primate biologist, wanted the rest of the chimps. She had nurtured orphaned chimps at a sanctuary in Zambia years before and understood the work. But the air force said no. They did not believe she could care for them.

Quickly, Dr. Noon started a nonprofit called Save the Chimps and started raising funds. Dr. Jane Goodall, the famed anthropologist and chimp expert, helped.

Some astronauts assisted too. Scott Carpenter, one of the Mercury Seven astronauts, and Buzz Aldrin, who walked on the Moon, wrote a protest letter to the air force. "I acknowledge and appreciate the enormous debt we owe the space chimpanzees," they began. "Now, it is time to repay this debt by giving these veterans the peaceful and permanent retirement they deserve."

The next year, Dr. Noon sued the air force on behalf of the chimpanzees. The judge gave her 21 chimps. She bought 150 acres of orange grove land in southern Florida to build island homes for them.

An Expensive Gift

In 2002 the Coulston Foundation offered to *give* Dr. Noon the rest of the air force chimps and their other research chimps. The catch? Dr. Noon had to *buy* their labs and land.

Dr. Noon raised more money, but her sanctuary couldn't accommodate 285 chimps overnight. Or even in a few months.

Over the next 10 years, Save the Chimps bought more land and built more island habitats. Dr. Noon combined the New Mexico chimps into family groups of 20 to 25. Some choices were simple. Each family needed a mix of males and females and a wide age range. Brothers, sisters, and other relatives often ended up together.

The chimps in each group also needed to like each other. For Dr. Noon, this part was easy. "Quite frankly, you watch how two chimps act behind the bars and then you can make a pretty good guess if they'll get along. Either they are fighting between the bars or they are playing. If they are playing and grooming, then you open the door. And that is pretty much the role of the human being. You open the door. The chimps walk through the door and do all the rest. . . . They are so ready to get on with their lives."

As workers finished each island, a new chimp family made the 2,000-mile-trip from New Mexico to Florida. Seven to ten chimps traveled in a 38-foot tractor trailer, each with a window seat and a peanut butter and jelly sandwich in hand. Forming families in New Mexico made the move easier for the chimps. The chimps may have moved to a new place, but they stayed with their friends.

Mercury astronaut Scott Carpenter and *Columbia* astronaut Robert Crippen toured the islands on golf carts. The chimps spat water at them, screamed, and barked. After the tour, Lieutenant Carpenter praised the astrochimps: "I have great respect for space travelers more senior than I, and I have great respect for the species that did it first."

Two of Minnie's children, Li'l Mini and Rebel, live together at Save the Chimps. Other astrochimp veterans also live there: Amy, Emily, Garfield, Liza, and

Tammy. The chimps play, gossip, and groom, just like wild chimps.

Fading Fame

Ham did not retire to Save the Chimps. He didn't live in a chimp family either. Instead, he still lived alone at the National Zoo.

Sergeant Dittmer and veterinarian Dr. Britz both visited Ham. Dr. Britz found the former astrochimp resting on a perch, chewing a piece of straw. "He glanced down, did a double-take, and jumped up and down in front of me. Ham was telling me that he knew me."

Reporters visited Ham for space events and anniversaries. For Ham's fifth space anniversary, zookeepers gave him a banana. He ate the peel first, then the fruit. When Americans went to the Moon and when the United States and the Soviet Union began a joint space mission in 1975, newspapers ran front-page stories about Ham.

When the astrochimp turned 20 in 1977, he had fallen to number five on the zoo's most popular list, behind the white tiger, the giant pandas, the monkeys, and the Smokey Bear exhibit. Maybe people wanted the young, cute space star from their memories, and not an aging chimp with gray muzzle hair.

Ham didn't do tricks for visitors anymore. "He lounges about on the floor with his feet up, does a little climbing, raises a racket at times, scratches himself, and enjoys being tickled by his keepers," said a zoo worker.

Ham drinking grapefruit juice from a bottle at the National Zoo in late 1973. Visitors were surprised to see how much their favorite astrochimp had aged. *NASA*

A Family for Ham

In 1980 Ham moved again. Les Schobert, the general curator of animals at the North Carolina Zoo in Asheboro, made a trade deal for him. Schobert didn't want just any chimpanzee, or a space star. He wanted Ham, and he wanted him to live more like a chimp, with a family.

Workers from the National Zoo drove Ham to the National Guard hangar at a nearby airport. A few dozen pilots stared at Ham, confused. Why were people treating this chimpanzee like a king? A brigadier general was flying his plane, for crying out loud. It made no sense.

Then someone explained this was Ham, America's first astronaut. *Ahhhh.* Quickly, a lieutenant organized a special send-off. The pilots lined up along the runway, saluting the astrochimp as he entered the plane.

North Carolina zookeepers met the plane on the runway and carried Ham's cage from the plane to their van. Ham bared his teeth, threatening the strangers. Where were they taking him? Back to Chimp College in New Mexico? Or the Miami Rare Bird Farm? Or Africa?

During his first month at the North Carolina Zoo, Ham lived in a tall cage, away from the other chimps. He heard their barks and whispers but couldn't see them.

After a few weeks, zookeepers moved Ham's cage. More than an acre of fluffy green grass and trees called out to his toes. Rocks and water bordered the habitat, not a wire fence. Scents from lions, baboons, elephants, and rhinos drifted by with the clouds. Ham studied his new family: two males, Hondo and Koby, and five females, Betty, Gracie, Maggie, Ruthie, and Terri. He touched their fingertips through the bars as they passed by.

A month later, zookeepers guided Maggie into Ham's cage. Experts rolled their eyes. A human-raised chimp such as Ham living with other chimpanzees? Never. Zookeepers sat nearby, taking notes.

Ham thrashed, hitting the wall and climbing the cage. Maggie screamed!

"When he went up the wire, Maggie came down, and vice versa," noted the keepers. "This behavior lasted only a minute, and then things calmed down."

Soon, the two chimps looked like old friends, playing games, chatting, and grooming. Zookeepers unlocked his cage, and America's first astronaut began a new life.

Ham and Maggie splashed through the stream, scooped ants from a termite mound, and played in the shade on a climbing gym. Sometimes, Gracie and Terrie joined them. Hondo tried spoiling the fun, showing off and picking fights. Zookeepers watched carefully. Hondo might not be bluffing, and Koby stayed at his side, egging him on. For Ham's safety, the zoo housed Hondo and Koby in different sleeping quarters.

Zookeepers visited the chimps a few times each day, bringing peanuts and Jell-O cubes for snacks. They squirted mustard and honey between branches, too, so the chimps could find their own treats. No one asked Ham to count or match shapes.

Zookeeper Debbie Mounts remembers Ham's early days in Asheboro. At night, keepers scattered food through the chimp area before bringing the chimps inside. (The scattered food gave everyone an equal chance at finding food.) Chimps chatted in glee each time they found a treat. "Ham seemed excited, too, but probably didn't know how to control it. He would rush in with his hair all bristled out with lots of stomping and running around, sometimes flinging the large rubber tubs and flakes of straw bedding. The other chimps got out of his way! Eventually, he would calm down. Everyone would enjoy their meal and settle in for the night."

Ham in his new outdoor habitat at the North Carolina Zoo.
Jim Page, North Carolina Department of Natural Resources and Community Development

As the months passed, Ham spent more time napping under the trees. Sometimes he raised his hairs and roared, telling the world he was boss. Sometimes he served as a peacemaker, breaking up fights and mending hurt feelings, like dominant chimps do in the wild.

At night, Ham listened to the lions. And stared up at the sky . . .

EPILOGUE

Today, using chimpanzees as astronauts sounds absurd. But many Americans didn't think clearly during the Space Race. They wanted space as America's territory.

Would the United States make the same choices now?

NASA engineer Robert Thompson tried to explain the past: "In today's mature world, we wouldn't do a lot of the things we did then, but a lot of the things we did then allowed us to move on quickly, much more quickly than we would today."

Soon after the human flights, the chimps' fame faded away. Most space movies and books do not mention the astrochimps. When they do talk about them, it's brief. Or they turn the chimps into cartoonlike characters.

Colonel John Glenn described the astrochimps' work as "a few simple tricks" in his autobiography. A few simple tricks? How many wild animals can count to fifty? Measure time? Learn colors and shapes?

As people learn more about animals' minds, it becomes more important to honor the astrochimps and protect chimps taken from the wild. Recently, a Japanese researcher showed that chimpanzees have more short-term memory than humans. In their forest homes, this helps chimps do two things at once, such as leaping through trees while watching for predators. During space training, these skills helped Vickie memorize all 72 shape questions.

Dr. Frans de Waal, a famous primatologist, notes that chimpanzees understand fairness. Some chimps refuse to accept treats unless their friends also get treats. Dr. De Waal wonders whether humans are smart enough to understand animal intelligence.

Many people want better lives for American chimps. Attorney Steven Wise argues personhood cases before the New York State Supreme Court. Wise believes people should not treat animals with high intelligence, such as the great apes, elephants, and whales, as things. They deserve the same nonhuman personhood rights that corporations enjoy. Animals with personhood rights could not do things like vote or drive cars, but laws would protect them from bad owners.

REST IN PEACE

Enos. About 10 months after his trip to space, Enos got a bacterial infection called shigella dysentery. (Shigella and salmonella infections are common in young chimps.) Enos moved to the Chimp College hospital, where veterinarians gave him antibiotics and IV fluids. He passed away two months later. No one knows where he was buried.

Ham. In January 1983, 22 years after his spaceflight, Ham died at the North Carolina Zoo from heart and liver disease. He was 26 years old, which is young for a captive chimp. Zookeepers found Maggie with him.

Ryita Price from the International Space Hall of Fame (now part of the New Mexico Museum of Space History) planned a funeral for Ham and invited Alan Shepard. "I don't know if you're an animal lover or not," she wrote, "or how much you feel our space program owes the primates who first proved man could survive space. I do know that you had to cope with a lot of jokes and sometimes 'unfunny' humor about the situation. And, perhaps, now would be a good time to give a timely and dignified response to those innuendoes and, at the same time, create some goodwill for the United States space program."

Alan Shepard wrote back to Price. No, he said, he couldn't come to Ham's funeral. He was too busy. The Hall of Fame displays both letters.

More than 50 people attended Ham's funeral, including Yolanda Martinez, the seamstress who made the astrochimp space suits. Ham's grave marks the entrance to the New Mexico Museum of Space History. Visitors often leave plastic and real bananas on his gravestone. His headstone reads:

World's First Astrochimp Ham
Born: 1955, Cameroons, Equatorial Africa
Died: 18 Jan. 1983, North Carolina Zoological Park, NC

Minnie. Minnie was the last original astrochimp when she died from a stroke in 1998 at age 41. In Minnie's obituary, the director of the New Mexico Museum of Space History said, "These chimpanzees were true pioneers and heroes of the space program."

GLOSSARY

astrochimps: A group of highly trained chimpanzees from the Mercury Chimpanzee Program; beta tested the space environment and technology for America's human astronauts; also called chimponauts.

beta tests: Early trials of new products or systems; designed to find problems that engineers and designers can fix.

booster rockets: Powerful rockets used to move spacecrafts from Earth's surface into space. America's suborbital flights used Redstone booster rockets, while America's orbital flights used Atlas booster rockets.

CapCom: The person assigned to relay information between the human astronaut in the space capsule and Mission Control; abbreviation for **cap**sule **com**municator.

centrifuges: Large machines used by NASA to train human and chimpanzee astronauts in simulated strong gravitational forces and sudden stops and starts.

cherry pickers: During the Space Race, a crane-like rig positioned at the launchpad to rescue astronauts from last-minute emergencies. A young boy invented the first cherry picker when he grew tired of climbing back up and down the ladder every time he moved to a new part of a tree.

chimponaut: One of the early names used for the astro-chimps; became less popular when language experts reminded people that its Greek translation meant "chimp sailor."

cosmonaut: The name used for Soviet astronauts; translates from the Greek to "sailor of the cosmos."

ECS (Environmental Control System): The technology developed by American scientists to provide human and chimpanzee astronauts with breathable oxygen, remove carbon dioxide and water vapor, and maintain a safe temperature while inside the spacecraft.

engineer: Someone who invents and tests machines or products using applied science. During the Space Race, engineers developed booster rockets, heat shields, breathing systems, and more.

gantry: Large metal structures placed on launchpads that give workers access to rockets and spacecrafts; can be equipped with pulleys, cranes, platforms, and elevators.

gravity: The force that pulls objects toward each other and gives them weight; often expressed as g-force.

Humans and chimpanzees who travel through space can face strong g-forces as they accelerate to high speeds; also see zero gravity.

Mercury Seven: America's first seven human astronauts.

Mission Control: A building or room filled with flight controllers who direct countdowns, liftoffs, and returns. Mission Control also collects and shares information from and with tracking stations, NASA officials, and the human astronaut(s).

orbital spaceflights: Space trips that orbit around Earth or another planet or moon; the astrochimp Enos made an orbital flight.

sanctuaries: Forever homes that provide high-quality food, housing, and medical care for animals without expecting them to perform for or interact with humans.

satellite: An object that orbits another object in space. Natural satellites include Earth, the Moon, and other planets and their moons. Human-made satellites collect and share weather data, move information for cell phone and Internet users, spy on people and countries, and more. Satellites range from very small, such as the Soviet Sputniks, to very large, such as the International Space Station.

splashdown: The moment an airborne spacecraft lands on or in water.

Soviet Union: The first Communist country; existed between 1922 to 1991; Russia was the largest of its 15 states.

Sputniks: Satellites launched by the Soviet Union during the Space Race that instilled fear and competition in the United States.

suborbital spaceflights: Spaceflights that enter low space but do not orbit Earth or another planet or moon; the astrochimp Ham made a suborbital flight.

zero gravity or zero g: A condition in which there is very little or no gravitational force exerted on an object; also called microgravity. During the early days of the Space Race, doctors and scientists were worried that $0\,g$ conditions in space could injure a chimpanzee or human astronaut.

AUTHOR'S NOTE

Many years ago, I discovered the astrochimps as a middle grader while on a field trip to the Kennedy Space Center in south Florida. An exhibit sign told Ham's story, but it seemed unbelievable. Decades later, while researching blood in space for another book, I rediscovered the astrochimps. Learning about their lives then and the lives of wild and captive chimpanzees today was an incredible adventure.

As often as possible, I studied primary sources and interviewed people who worked with the astrochimps. Dr. William Britz, Dr. Vernon Pegram, Willie Ogden, Jennifer Hoyle, Dr. Scott Kenward, Melanie Bond, Jenn Ireland, and Debbie Mounts generously shared their time and insights.

Information from NASA reports, oral histories, the John F. Kennedy Presidential Library and Museum, the Johnson Space Center, the National Archives, and the Smithsonian National Air and Space Museum formed the research backbone for this story. Librarians and museum archivists provided materials and leads. Specifically, I would like to thank Jim Mayberry at the New Mexico Museum of Space History, Diane Villa at the North Carolina Zoo, and Heidi Stover at the Smithsonian Archives.

Books, magazines, news stories, and documentaries from the following writers, historians, scientists, and media groups were also invaluable: Clyde R. Bergwin, Ed Blair, Colin Burgess, M. Scott Carpenter, John Catchpole, William Coleman, Frans de Waal, Jane Goodall, Deborah Hadfield, Dave Karten, Gene Kranz, George Meeter, Mary Roach, Asif Siddiqi, Deke Slayton, Reginald Turnill, Guenter Wendt, Tom Wolfe, *Life* magazine, *National Geographic*, United Press International, and the Associated Press.

Working on this project required unraveling some urban legends. Many sources state that Ham was named after his space trip, and that his name was an acronym for Holloman Aerospace Medical Center. However, national newspapers ran a photo of Ham three months before his flight wearing a space suit with HAM (not HAM) on it. Ham was likely named for base commander Lieutenant Colonel Hamilton Blackshear, who went by the nickname Ham.

In the early 1970s, traveling chimp shows claimed Ham, "America's First Astronaut," as their star. (The real Ham lived at the National Zoo and did not perform in shows or TV commercials.)

In 2002 someone added a Wikipedia entry about Ham starring in a movie with Evel Knievel, the famous motorcycle stunt artist. The writer was not trying to lie; they just misunderstood something they read on another website. A few years later, two authors used the false Wikipedia page as a source for their book about space animals. Then, someone added the book to the Wikipedia page as a citation. People still mention Ham's adventure with Evel Knievel, citing Wikipedia and the book as sources!

Other urban legends about the astrochimps say Minnie was the runner-up for both the suborbital *and* the orbital flights. NASA reports do not list Minnie as one of the five flight-ready chimps sent to Cape Canaveral for the orbital mission. Some sources also say that four females and two males went to Cape Canaveral for the suborbital trip. Veterinarian Bill Britz confirms that only one female, Minnie, went to the Cape.

RESOURCES

Chimpanzee Sanctuaries

Poachers took most astrochimps from their forest homes in the late 1950s and early 1960s. But do people treat chimpanzees any better today? Wild chimps are still poached for the exotic pet trade and hunted for bushmeat. And every time people clear-cut a forest to make room for more human houses and farmland, chimps lose their food and shelter. In many villages, humans and chimpanzees do not get along. Farmers rage at chimps who eat their sugarcane and fruits, while families worry that hungry chimps may hurt their children.

In some countries, including the United States, it's still legal to buy chimpanzees for pets. Young chimps may look super cute and fun, but adults are more than *seven times stronger* than humans. When people give away their pet chimps, the chimps feel sad and abandoned. They often don't bond well with other chimps.

Today, companies face pressure to stop using chimps in movies, commercials, and carnivals. These uses create buyers for young chimps poached from the wild. Studies also show that people are less likely to believe animals need protection when they see endangered species on TV.

The chimpanzee sanctuaries below care for chimps who need homes. Some sanctuaries are not open to visitors, but others allow donors to see the chimps once or twice a year. Many sanctuaries share stories and videos that let online visitors meet their chimps.

Save the Chimps, Fort Pierce, Florida
https://savethechimps.org

Project Chimps, Blue Ridge, Georgia
https://projectchimps.org

**Chimpanzee Sanctuary Northwest,
Cle Elum, Washington**
https://chimpsnw.org/

Chimp Haven, Keithville, Louisiana
https://chimphaven.org

Fauna Foundation, Carignan, Québec
https://faunafoundation.org

Center for Great Apes, Wauchula, Florida
https://centerforgreatapes.org

Ways to Honor, Ways to Care

Remembering the world's Space Race animals may be the best way to honor them. Ten years ago, the Russians crafted a statue of their first space dog, Laika, standing on a rocket near her launchpad. And fans of the French space cat Félicette raised money to build a bronze sculpture of the feline and her rocket.

Here are a few ways to honor the astrochimps:

★ Raise money for chimpanzee sanctuaries. They use donations to buy food, medicines, and toys.
★ Start a Jane Goodall Roots & Shoots group, and choose a project that will help chimpanzees. See https://rootsandshoots.org.
★ Nominate your favorite astrochimps to the International Space Hall of Fame at the New Mexico Museum of Space History. The Hall of Fame honors people who advanced space science, including the Mercury Seven astronauts and the Russian cosmonauts Yuri Gagarin and Gherman Titov. It also inducted other members of the Mercury program, including Sergeant Ed Dittmer, Pad Leader Guenter Wendt, the

astronauts' doctor, and the spacecraft's design engineer. The astrochimps also deserve this honor. Send signed petitions to P.O. Box 5430, Alamogordo, NM 88311-5430, Attention: Hall of Fame Nomination Committee.

★ Organize a petition for Enos to receive a grave marker near Ham. Mail the petition to P.O. Box 5430, Alamogordo, NM 88311-5430.

Space Centers and Museums

If you don't have a road trip planned any time soon, check out the websites for virtual adventures!

Kennedy Space Center, Cape Canaveral, Florida

https://www.kennedyspacecenter.com
Wander through the Rocket Garden to compare the Mercury and Atlas rockets, which sent Ham and Enos to space, to larger booster rockets that powered America to the Moon and Mars. Climb the launchpad towers for a great view of the Cape, check out Mars rovers, and play interactive games.

New Mexico Museum of Space History, Alamogordo, New Mexico

https://www.nmspacemuseum.org
Just down the road from Holloman Air Force Base, this museum features astrochimp couches, lever panels, and Ham's space uniform and flight jacket. Ham's burial plaque marks the entrance.

Smithsonian National Air and Space Museum, Washington, DC, and Chantilly, Virginia

https://airandspace.si.edu/visit

Reserve a virtual field trip or planetarium show, check out spacecrafts and rocket engines up close, and discover experiments and games to build flight and physics skills.

Space Center Houston and NASA Johnson Space Center, Houston, Texas

https://spacecenter.org/visitor-information/

Take a NASA Tram Tour of astronaut training facilities, the Mission Control center that monitors the International Space Station, and Rocket Park. Search the Starship Gallery for astrochimp artifacts, and climb aboard a space shuttle replica and its carrier aircraft.

Virginia Air & Space Center, Hampton, Virginia

https://www.visitnasa.com/virginia-air-space-center

Ready for hands-on action? Step inside simulators to program a Mars robot and pilot a plane or the space shuttle. Check out the machine used to train American astronauts to land on the Moon, a meteorite from Mars, and much more.

Jet Propulsion Laboratory, Pasadena, California

https://www.visitnasa.com/jet-propulsion
-laboratory-california

Discover the world of exoplanets, enjoy Near-Earth Watches of asteroids and comets, explore space robotics, make Mars helicopters, and go on virtual tours with your school. If you visit in person, don't miss the Space-craft Assembly Facility.

US Space & Rocket Center, Huntsville, Alabama

https://www.visitnasa.com/us-space-rocket
-center-alabama

If virtual reality and hands-on experiences rock your world, this is the space center for you. Enjoy weekend astronaut training programs, flight simulators, under-water walking, and scuba classes. History buffs will enjoy the Rocket Center.

Morehead Planetarium and Science Center, Chapel Hill, North Carolina

http://moreheadplanetarium.org

Visit the planetarium where the Mercury Seven astro-nauts practiced their space geography skills. Multimedia and live star shows explore human space travel, stars, skies, the solar system, dark matter, and more.

NOTES

1. WILD LIVES

"A lot of things": Edward C. Dittmer, "New Mexico Museum of Space History Oral History Project," interview by George M. House, April 29, 1987, as reproduced in Curation Paper Number Eight, Summer 2012, page 11.

"Chimps that came from": Bill Britz, in discussion with the author, January 17, 2018.

"One night, one of the chimps": Britz, discussion.

"But I never saw": Britz, discussion.

"We had to be careful not": Jordan Schraeder, "Cold War Monkey Business," *Alcalde: The Official Publication of the Texas Exes*, January/February 2012, https://alcalde .texasexes.org/2012/01/cold-war-monkey-business/.

"But that didn't last": Britz, discussion.

"Some chimps paid a lot": Britz, discussion.

"waving and jabbering": Harold R. Williams, "High Flyer Given Much Training," *Hobbs (NM) Daily News*, February 5, 1961, https://www.newspapers.com/image/legacy/35154792/.

"We would set them about": Dittmer, "New Mexico Museum," 12.

"Finally, we could set them": Dittmer, "New Mexico Museum," 12.

"Let me tell you": "Chimps No Chumps, UK Finds," *Cincinnati Enquirer*, December 5, 1961, https://www.newspapers.com/image/legacy/104612742/.

"one of the lucky trainers": Vernon Pegram, in discussion with the author, January 19, 2019.

"It was a mild shock": Britz, discussion.

"Vickie looked like she": Britz, discussion.

"If you gave Vickie": Britz, discussion.

"One day" says Dr. Britz, "Dr. Fineg": Britz, discussion.

"going faster and faster": Pegram, discussion.

"You were straining every muscle": John Glenn, *John Glenn: A Memoir* (New York: Bantam, 1999), 278.

"Many times," Wendt wrote: Guenter Wendt and Russell Still, *The Unbroken Chain* (Burlington, ON: Apogee Books/Collector's Guide Publishing, 2001), 21.

"During one particularly long": Wendt and Still, *Unbroken Chain*, 21.

"There is no discrimination": Erik Bergaust, "Is Space a Place for the Ladies?," *Birmingham News*, September

2, 1962, https://www.newspapers.com/image/legacy /575003829/.

"I was going to the Cape": Claiborne R. Hicks, "NASA Johnson Space Center Oral History Project: Claiborne R. Hicks," interview by Kevin M. Rusnak, April 11, 2000, https://historycollection.jsc.nasa.gov /JSCHistoryPortal/history/oral_histories/HicksCR /HicksCR_4-11-00.htm.

"Wham! *It just blew up.*": Donald "Deke" K. Slayton, *Deke! U.S. Manned Space: From Mercury to the Shuttle* (New York: Forge, 1994), 89.

"went berserk over the Florida sky": Titash Sen, "The Time Machine: The Story Behind the Man on the Moon," *The Wire*, July 20, 2017, https://thewire.in/history /neil-armstrong-buzz-aldrin-man-on-the-moon.

"I've been a pilot": Tom Wolfe, *The Right Stuff* (New York: Picador, 1979), 100. See also Walter Spearman, "The Literary Lantern," *Durham Sun*, October 27, 1979, https:// www.newspapers.com/image/legacy/787441617/.

"a great circus act": Alan Shepard and Deke Slayton, *Moon Shot* (Atlanta: Turner Publishing, 1994), 89, 82.

"The human astronauts did not": Britz, discussion.

"I don't want to fly anything": Christian Williams, "Pilot Broke Sound Barrier in '47, Hasn't Slowed Down," *Los Angeles Times*, October 29, 1981, https://www .newspapers.com/newspage/388315112.

"assailed by hoots, screeches": Shepard and Slayton, *Moon Shot*, 87.

"In the end": Alan Shepard, "First Step to the Moon," *American Heritage*, July/August 1994, https://www .americanheritage.com/first-step-moon.

"One day," says Dr. Britz, "we took Minnie": Britz, discussion.

2. ASTROCHIMPS IN SPACE

"The suborbital flights": John Glenn, "Interview with Astronaut John H. Glenn, Jr.," interview by Robert Stevens, in "First U.S. Man in Orbit," pt. 3, https:// catalog.archives.gov/id/278178.

"We could handle": Wayne E. Koons, "NASA Johnson Space Center Oral History Project Edited Oral History Transcript: Wayne E. Koons," interview by Rebecca Wright, October 14, 2004, https://history collection.jsc.nasa.gov/JSCHistoryPortal/history /oral_histories/KoonsWE/KoonsWE_10-14-04.htm.

"The third stop": Koons, "NASA Johnson Space Center."

"monster": Guenter F. Wendt, "NASA Johnson Space Center Oral History Project Edited Oral History Transcript: Guenter F. Wendt," interview by Catherine Harwood, February 25, 1999, https://historycollection .jsc.nasa.gov/JSCHistoryPortal/history/oral_histories /WendtG/WendtG_2-25-99.htm.

"I had been down there": Dittmer, "New Mexico Museum," 14.

"We sat there waiting": Britz, discussion.

"We've got it": Koons, "NASA Johnson Space Center."

"We were assuming the ship": Koons, "NASA Johnson Space Center."

"At this point," said Lieutentant Koons: Koons, "NASA Johnson Space Center."

"a very heavy spacecraft": Koons, "NASA Johnson Space Center."

"a cross between a kitten's meow": Frank Carey, "Space Chimpanzee Rides Back in Style." *Stevens Point (WI) Journal*, February 2, 1961, https://www.newspapers.com/image/legacy/251108573.

"He's talking to us": Carey, "Space Chimpanzee Rides."

"turned his head from": Carey, "Space Chimpanzee Rides."

"Ham looks serenely": John Beckler, "Ham, the Chimpanzee, Hams It Up as Motion Picture Star," *Montana Standard*, February 9, 1961, https://www.newspapers.com/image/legacy/354365881.

"The hatch was opened": Joseph V. Brady, "Conversation with Joseph V. Brady," interview, *Addiction* 100, no. 12 (December 2005): 1805–12, https://onlinelibrary.wiley.com/doi/10.1111/j.1360-0443.2005.01246.x.

"I didn't know if he": Betty Jo Canter, "A 21 Story Salute: Nursing Experiences in Harm's Way During World War II, Korea and Vietnam," Minerd.com, accessed August 31, 2022, https://www.minerd.com/memoir-a21storysalute.htm.

"Boy," said the sergeant: Dittmer, "New Mexico Museum," 14.

"I'm sure glad that little fellow": Clyde R. Bergwin and William T. Coleman, *Animal Astronauts: They Opened the*

Way to the Stars (Englewood Cliffs, NJ: Prentice-Hall, 1963), 172.

"The hoses were connected": Robert F. Thompson, "NASA Johnson Space Center Oral History Project Edited Oral History Transcipt: Robert F. Thompson," interview by Jennifer Ross-Nazzal, December 30, 2002, https://historycollection.jsc.nasa.gov/JSCHistory Portal/history/oral_histories/SamonskiFH /SamonskiFH_12-30-02.htm.

"It turns out, as we reconstructed": Robert F. Thompson, *Oral History Transcript*, interview by Kevin M. Rusnak, August 29, 2000, https://historycollection.jsc .nasa.gov/JSCHistoryPortal/history/oral_histories /ThompsonRF/RFT_8-29-00.pdf.

"I find it amazing that Ham": Pegram, discussion.

"a big flash of sunlight": C. Frederick Matthews, "NASA Johnson Space Center Oral History Project Edited Oral History Transcript: C. Frederick Matthews," interview by Rebecca Wright, June 23, 1999, https://history collection.jsc.nasa.gov/JSCHistoryPortal/history/oral _histories/MatthewsCF/MatthewsCF_6-23-99.htm.

"Our preliminary studies lead us": "Man Could Have Survived Ham's Flight, Expert Says," *Portland Press Herald*, February 4, 1961, https://www.newspapers .com/image/legacy/847852868/.

"I certainly didn't blame him": Pegram, discussion.

"The only reason": John B. Lee, "NASA Johnson Space Center Oral History Project Edited Oral History Transcript: John B. Lee," interview by Jennifer Ross-Nazzal,

January 16, 2008, https://historycollection.jsc.nasa
.gov/JSCHistoryPortal/history/oral_histories/LeeJB
/LeeJB_1-16-08.htm.

"Chipper Chimp Gives Go-Ahead": Alton Blakeslee,
"Chimp's Survival Gives Go-Ahead to Manned
Flight," *Sunbury Daily Item*, February 1, 1961, https://
www.newspapers.com/image/legacy/512266170/.

"Chimp Trip Prelude for Spacemen": "Chimp Trip Prelude for Spacemen," *Evening Standard*, February 1,
1961, https://www.newspapers.com/image/legacy
/27693896/.

"The Soviet press and radio": "Soviets Give Ham
Unusual Prominence," *Charlotte Observer*, February 2, 1961, https://www.newspapers.com/image
/legacy/619975161/.

"Rocket Ride Film Shows": Associated Press, "Rocket Ride
Film Shows Ham in Ham," *Arizona Daily Star*, February 10, 1961, https://www.newspapers.com/image
/legacy/166384373/.

"The irony of playing": Shepard, "First Step to the Moon."

"I guess they ran out": Colin Burgess, *Friendship 7: The Epic
Orbital Flight of John H. Glenn, Jr.* (New York: Springer,
2015), 27.

"We would joke about": Jule Hubbard, "Part of Space
Program History," *Wilkes Journal-Patriot*, September
3, 2012, https://www.journalpatriot.com/news/part
-of-space-program-history/article_3ec7de6c-f5e4-11e1
-be6c-0019bb30f31a.html.

"hit it with waves": Thompson, *Oral History Transcript*.

"It turned out that you": Robert B. Voas, "NASA Johnson Space Center Oral History Project Edited Oral History Transcript: Dr. Robert B. Voas," interview by Summer Chick Bergen, May 19, 2002, https://history collection.jsc.nasa.gov/JSCHistoryPortal/history /oral_histories/VoasRB/VoasRB_5-19-02.htm.

"When Yuri Gagarin flew": Maxime A. Faget, "NASA Johnson Space Center Oral History Project Edited Oral History Transcript: Maxime A. Faget," interview by Jim Slade, June 18 and 19, 1997, https://history collection.jsc.nasa.gov/JSCHistoryPortal/history /oral_histories/FagetMA/FagetMA_6-18-97.htm.

"particularly pleased to receive Pushinka": John F. Kennedy to Nikita Khrushchev, Department of State, Presidential Correspondence, Lot 66 D 204, https://history .state.gov/historicaldocuments/frus1961-63v06/d17.

"Maybe [NASA] should make": Bernard Kahn, "I Flew with Alan Shepard," *Daytona Beach Morning Journal*, February 7, 1971, https://books.google.com /books?id=7k0fAAAAIBAJ&printsec=frontcover& source.

"Visions of exploding rockets": Wendt and Still, *Unbroken Chain*, 34.

"Gordoooooo . . .": Wendt and Still, *Unbroken Chain*, 34.

"At this point I could look": Jerome B. Hammack et al., eds., "Postlaunch Report for Mercury-Redstone No. 3 (MR-3)" (working paper no. 192, Space Task Group, National Aeronautics and Space Administration,

Langley Field, Virginia, June 16, 1961), 53, https://history.nasa.gov/PostlaunchMR3.pdf.

"kept thinking about": Shepard, "First Step to the Moon."

"We had been given some warnings": Koons, "NASA Johnson Space Center."

"You don't have to be": Dan Brown, "You, Too, Can Take a Whirl Through Space," *Miami Herald*, May 7, 1961, https://www.newspapers.com/image/legacy/619539061/.

"That little race between": NASA, *Astronaut Alan B. Shepard, Jr., May 5, 1961*, color print, May 5, 1961, last updated August 7, 2017, NASA, https://www.nasa.gov/multimedia/imagegallery/image_feature_1076.html.

"landing a man on the Moon": John F. Kennedy, "Address to the Joint Session of Congress," May 25, 1961, https://www.jfklibrary.org/node/16986.

"This was really the first time": Robert R. Gilruth, "Oral History Interview with Robert R. Gilruth," interview by Walter D. Sohier, April 1, 1964, John F. Kennedy Oral History Program, https://www.jfklibrary.org/sites/default/files/archives/JFKOH/Gilruth%2C%20Robert%20R/JFKOH-RRG-01/JFKOH-RRG-01-TR.pdf.

3. RACING TO DEEPER SPACE

"absorb the growing heat": Wendt and Still, *Unbroken Chain*, 14.

"Its skin was so thin": Wendt and Still, *Unbroken Chain*, 42.

"The cutoff speed and angle": Glenn, "Interview with Astronaut John H. Glenn."

"The stations pass [the spacecraft]": Scott M. Carpenter, et al., *We Seven* (New York: Simon and Schuster, 1962), 295.

"You have made yourself immortal": "Science: The Cruise of the Vostok," *Time*, April 21, 1961, https://content.time .com/time/subscriber/article/0,33009,895299-2,00.html.

"more than 90 percent of the monitored": Central Intelligence Agency, *The Soviet Bioastronautics Research Program* (n.p.: Central Intelligence Agency, 1962) 39, https:// www.cia.gov/readingroom/docs/DOC_0001344000 .pdf.

"We will not have to wait": Eugene M. Emme, *Aeronautical and Astronautical Events of 1961*, report of the National Aeronautics and Space Administration to the Committee on Science and Astronautics, US House of Representatives, 87th Cong., 2d. Sess. (Washington, DC: Government Printing Office, 1962), 1–13, https:// history.nasa.gov/AAchronologies/1961version2.pdf.

"Mercury manned satellite program": James Barr, "Is Mercury Program Headed for Disaster?," *Missiles and Rockets*, August 15, 1960, quoted in Loyd S. Swenson, James M. Grimwood, and Charles C. Alexander, *This New Ocean: A History of Project Mercury* (Washington, DC: National Aeronautics and Space Administration, NASA History Division, 1998), https://archive.org /stream/thisnewoceanhist00swen/thisnewocean hist00swen_djvu.txt.

"Some letter writers to NASA": Kenneth Sheibel, "Target Date Draws Near," *Courier-News*, April 12, 1961, https://www.newspapers.com/image/legacy/2188 41767/.

"The destruction of the Mercury-Atlas 3": Gene Kranz, *Failure Is Not an Option* (New York: Simon & Schuster, 2000), 41.

"If we are to have our spectacular": "Spectacular Failures Ahead, Webb Warns," *Intelligencer Journal* (Lancaster, PA), May 9, 1961, https://www.newspapers.com /image/legacy/558026141/.

"canned man" was "really much better": Faget, "NASA Johnson Space Center."

"The MA-5 mission is more than": Bergwin and Coleman, *Animal Astronauts*, 158.

"Ham, the chimpanzee who blazed": Howard Benedict, "Trail-Blazing Chimpanzee May Get 2nd Space Flight," *Morning Call* (Allentown, PA), November 7, 1961, https://www.newspapers.com/image/legacy /275245144/.

"all in good health": Dave Karten, "New Ventures for AF Vets," *The Speculum* 15, no. 3 (Spring 1962): 6–12, https://kb.osu.edu/bitstream/handle/1811/44841 /SPECULUM_v15_i03_1962_low.pdf?sequence=3.

"Of the many factors which may affect": Frederick H. Rohles, et al., *A Laboratory Model for a Fourteen Day Orbital Flight with a Chimpanzee* (Holloman Air Force Base, NM: Air Force Missile Development Center, United States Air Force, October 1961).

"one of the most excitable animals": John D. Mosely and James P. Henry, "Summary of the Results of the MA-5 Flight," in *Results of the Project Mercury Ballistic and Orbital Chimpanzee Flights*, eds. James P. Henry and John D. Mosely (Houston, TX: NASA Manned Spacecraft Center, 1963), 69, https://history.nasa.gov /SP39Chimpanzee.pdf.

"moody and a little indifferent": "Knew Enos When . . . a Bum Student," *Detroit Free Press*, January 12, 1961, https://www.newspapers.com/image/legacy /98602506/.

"Enos was a good chimp": Dittmer, "New Mexico Museum," 13.

"Just getting Enos into": Edward C. Dittmer, in discussion with the author, November 19, 2019.

"I told them they weren't monkeys": Wendt and Still, *Unbroken Chain*, 18. Wendt told this story many times over the years with slight variations.

"quietly and thoughtfully": Carpenter et al., *We Seven*, 294.

The chimpanzee *"reports that everything"*: John F. Kennedy, "Press Conference, 29 November 1961," State Department Auditorium, Washington, DC, audio, 32:26, https://www.jfklibrary.org/archives/other-resources /john-f-kennedy-press-conferences/news-conference -19.

"All sites, this is Cape Flight": Chris Kraft, *Flight: My Life in Mission Control* (New York: Dutton/Penguin Putnam, 2001), 151.

"All sites, monitor and report": Kraft, *Flight*, 151.

"Retrofire on my mark . . . four, three, two": Kraft, *Flight*, 152.

"In those last minutes": Kraft, *Flight*, 153.

"When he got back to the ground": G. Merritt Preston, "NASA Johnson Space Center Oral History Project Edited Oral History Transcript: G. Merritt Preston," interview by Carol Butler, February 1, 2000, https:// historycollection.jsc.nasa.gov/JSCHistoryPortal/history /oral_histories/PrestonGM/PrestonGM_2-1-00.htm.

"Go to the kitchen": Willie Ogden, in discussion with the author, June 17, 2021.

"Enos showed himself": "Enos Meets Press—No Monkey-shines," *Detroit Free Press*, December 1, 1961, https:// www.newspapers.com/image/legacy/98602506/.

"fended off the press": "Enos: A Cool Ape Ace," *Life*, December 8, 1961.

"I knew I'd never see him again": Ogden, discussion.

"I didn't train Enos": Ogden, discussion.

"I have talked to people": John Glenn, "I'll Have to Hit a Keyhole in the Sky," *Life*, December 8, 1961.

"following a chimp": Glenn, *John Glenn*, 323.

"We're a little behind the Russians": John Fischetti, "We're a Little Behind the Russians and a Little Ahead of the Americans," cartoon, *The Norman (OK) Transcript*, December 6, 1961, https://www.newspapers.com /image/legacy/602800926/.

"I will say it again and again": Ron Wilson, "Research That Launched Careers," *Norton (KS) Telegram*, August 30,

2013, http://www.nwkansas.com/nctwebpages/pdf %20pages%20-%20all/nt%20pages-pdfs%202013 /nt%20pages:08%20Aug/Week%205/Friday/03%20 8-30-13%202%20News.pdf.

"joked about taking along": "Glenn Says Normal Food OK in Space," *Times Recorder* (Zanesville, OH), April 7, 1962, https://www.newspapers.com/image/legacy /294181709/.

"Boy, that was a real fireball": Wayne Fuson, "A Real Fireball," *Indianapolis News*, February 26, 1962, https:// www.newspapers.com/image/legacy/312080531/.

"Where's the monkey?": "Glenn Terms Flight Just Step in Era," *Macon (GA) Telegraph*, February 27, 1962, https:// www.newspapers.com/image/legacy/826991629/.

4. BATTLE OF THE ASTRONAUTS

"I alienated some of the flight": Walter M. Schirra Jr., "NASA Johnson Space Center Oral History Project Edited Oral History Transcript: Walter M. Schirra, Jr.," interview by Roy Neal, December 1, 1998, https:// historycollection.jsc.nasa.gov/JSCHistoryPortal /history/oral_histories/SchirraWM/SchirraWM _12-1-98.htm.

5. ASTROCHIMPS ON THE MOON?

"If this were just a peaceful game": "How Big Is the 'Space Gap' Now?," *Tucson Daily Citizen*, August 15, 1962, https://www.newspapers.com/image/legacy /14926151/.

"Chimponaut May Be 1st": "Chimponaut May Be 1st to Plant Flag on Moon," *Orlando Sentinel*, June 17, 1962, https://www.newspapers.com/image/legacy/223329441/.

"read his press clippings": "Enos-the-Chimp, Space Pioneer, Dies at Holloman," *Albuquerque Journal*, November 6, 1962, https://www.newspapers.com/image/legacy/157926890/.

"pilot a spacecraft back": Harold Williams, "Chimps at Air Force College Learn to Pilot Space Ships," *Green Bay Press-Gazette*, December 14, 1963, https://www.newspapers.com/image/legacy/189299620/.

"There is no question about it": Williams, "Chimps at Air Force College."

"Bobby Joe knew what he wanted": Williams, "Chimps at Air Force College."

"highly sought-after assignment": Britz, discussion.

"too excited and unruly": Lillian Levy, "Animals Aiding Research for Manned Space Flight," *The Times* (Shreveport, LA), December 25, 1960, https://www.newspapers.com/image/legacy/214231860/.

"We could have flown her": *Mercury 13*, directed by David Sington and Heather Walsh (Los Gatos, CA: Netflix, 2018).

"Adult chimps can be seven times": Pegram, discussion.

"Chimps can wade but": Pegram, discussion.

"The problem in blasting": George Nobbe, "The Air Force Goes Ape," *Daily News* (New York), October 9, 1966, https://www.newspapers.com/newspage/461839222/.

6. FINAL FLIGHTS

"strutted and posed": Larry Bingham, "Uncertain Sanctuary," *Fort Worth Star-Telegram*, January 3, 1999, https://www.newspapers.com/image/648691857/?terms=primarily%20primates%20strutted%20and%20posed&match=1.

"I acknowledge and appreciate": Cliff Rothman, "Giving Chimps Their Space," *Los Angeles Times*, August 6, 1998, https://www.newspapers.com/image/160153339.

"Quite frankly, you watch": Carole Noon, "Opening the Door: Save the Chimps Gives New Life to Florida Retirement," interview by Sangamithra Iyer, *Satya*, November/December 2004, http://www.satyamag.com/nov04/noon.html.

"I have great respect for": "STC Welcomes NASA Space Program," Save the Chimps (website), May 29, 2009, https://savethechimps.org/stc-welcomes-nasa-space-program/.

"He glanced down": Britz, discussion.

"He lounges about on": "Space Chimpanzee to Get New Home," *Colorado Springs Gazette-Telegraph*, September 1, 1977, https://www.newspapers.com/image/legacy/66217380/.

"When he went up the wire": Frye Gaillard, "A Space Pioneer Gets to Rejoin His Kind in N.C.," *Philadelphia Inquirer*, August 8, 1981, https://www.newspapers.com/image/legacy/173826804/.

"Ham seemed excited": Debbie Mounts, in discussion with the author, March 17, 2022.

EPILOGUE

"In today's mature world": Thompson, *Oral History Transcript*.

REST IN PEACE

"I don't know if you're": Ryita Price to Alan Shepard, February 8, 1983, New Mexico Museum of Space History, Alamogordo, New Mexico.

"These chimpanzees were true": Associated Press, "Last Space Chimp Dies at 41," *Albuquerque Journal*, March 28, 1998, https://www.newspapers.com/image/legacy/156955718/.

INDEX

Page numbers in *italics* refer to pictures and figures.